JERUSALEM | ROCK OF AGES

Frontispiece
View of the Old City from Abu Tor

JERUSALEM
ROCK OF AGES

Photographs by *ALFRED BERNHEIM* and *Ricarda Schwerin*

Text by FOSCO MARAINI   *Translated by Judith Landry*

A HELEN AND KURT WOLFF BOOK / HARCOURT, BRACE & WORLD, INC., NEW YORK

CONTENTS

In memory of my ever-present dead: my wife, my son

A. B.

JERUSALEM | ROCK OF AGES

I | NAVEL OF THE WORLD

How does a stone compare with a man?

As nothing, a bit of solidified sand, concentrated lime, variously crystallized mineral. Men gather stones from river beds, they quarry stone from mountains, use it to make walls, houses, basins, columns, towers, floors, bridges, tombstones, statues; they also break it up, burn it, turn it into mortar. Stone proposes, man disposes. Man commands, stone becomes.

On the other hand, how does man compare with stone?

As a passing fable, a cloud at dawn; hurtling from cradle to grave. His frail and sensitive flesh gathers the rarest and the most common elements from earth and air, fuses them, and organizes them into an extraordinary being which is capable of work, struggle, thought, love, dance, joy, hatred, which is woven of memories and hopes and is then lost again to the four, or six, corners of space. But stone remains. Stone can truly say: I exist, I remain. Millennia fall upon it like the dew.

In Jerusalem man and stone meet, converge. The stones of Jerusalem are scored with contact with men, and here men sign themselves in stone. The stones of Jerusalem are no ordinary stones; each one has a past that may have been dramatic and terrible; if they could speak, they would tell not only of crystallization and erosion, like those of rivers and mountains, but also of tears and the warmth of bodies, sometimes of merrymaking, more often of what men have shrieked out *in extremis*.

The stones of other ancient cities too—Athens, Rome, Benares, Mexico City—are steeped in history; but one has the impression that in Jerusalem there have been more frequent transformations, that time has eaten and digested them with greater eagerness. Jerusalem has been destroyed, rebuilt, shattered, and re-created so often that, if we could see it filmed in frames shot at the rate of one a year and then projected at the usual speed, the result would be like that of a city having an epileptic seizure.

Stones are the atoms in this convulsion, in this vortex: those beautiful pale gold stones which seem saturated with the light and heat of the sun, and which Alfred Bernheim and Ricarda Schwerin have photographed with such love and insight.

But Jerusalem is not made simply of men and of stones; there is a whole dimension which borders on the invisible and which makes this city unique. Men, stones, God: these are the terms of an immensely rich, profound, and complex picture.

The unity of a supreme Absolute which governs us all in some mysterious way is sensed, disclosed, proclaimed in many parts of the earth and at many moments in history. One need consider only Greek thought in its maturity, the intuitions of

Zoroaster, the sacred formula of the Indian rishi, the Tao of the Chinese masters, and Zen, and the celestial Buddhas of the Mahayana sects; but Jerusalem saw the birth, flowering, and growth of a special concept of God as a person, with whom we are linked by precise contractual and affective ties. If the stones of Jerusalem dance and whirl through the centuries, manipulated time and time again by men, the men of Jerusalem in their turn upset one another, love one another, kill and torment one another throughout millennia—inspired, driven, often almost broken by the idea of God, by opposing interpretations of the idea of God.

The main faiths alive in the world today should not be seen as a string of names, but as organic constellations of intuitions and thoughts which have evolved in time, of particular attitudes toward life, death, the cosmos, the running of public affairs, work, sex, beauty, suffering, the occult, the whole range of things affecting human existence. By extreme simplification it is possible to recognize three families: one linked with India, in the various forms of Hinduism, in the numerous Buddhist schools, in Jainism and several other lesser faiths; that of the Far East, characterized by the ethnic religions of China and Japan; and lastly the monotheist Semitic family. Today half the world is in some way the spiritual descendant of Abraham, because Jewish, Christian, and Islamic societies stem from him and his primordial mono-theism.

Admittedly, statistics are not to be trusted. What are we to understand when we read that there are nearly a billion Christians? Who has been sounding out the minds and hearts of the individual? Probably three quarters of them are—as Toynbee would say—post-Christians or ex-Christians. But over the centuries collective trans-missible values are formed in all societies, and these affect everyone, independently of the faith of the individual, and are crystallized in language and custom. It is in this sense that, even today, there still exist Christian, Jewish, and Islamic societies, and in no uncertain terms. And in this sense 1,500 millions of people do carry within them deep and hidden links with Abraham. And therefore, with Jerusalem, a true living symbol of the basic and genetic unity of the three monotheistic faiths.

A brief visit to the Haram-ash-Sharif ("Noble Sanctuary") is most enlightening. On this great esplanade full of sun and sky, which today houses one of the main Islamic shrines, the Dome of the Rock, third in importance after Mecca and Medina, three thousand years ago there stood the great Jewish Temple of Solomon. The Baby-lonians destroyed it (587 B.C.) but it was soon rebuilt by Zerubbabel. From 20 B.C. Herod renovated it so radically that one could really speak of a third Temple, the one that was the splendor of Jerusalem at the time of Jesus, and was destroyed by the Romans in A.D. 70.

Today the lack of points of reference makes one forget how sacred the place is to the memories of the drama of Christ. It was here, in the Temple, that Mary and

4

Joseph presented their recently born son (Luke 2:22) and here, in the Temple, that the boy Jesus disputed with the doctors (Luke 2:46). Later, as an adult, he spent whole days within the Temple precincts teaching and preaching (Luke 19:47). Here he spoke of matters such as authority, answered questions on paying tribute, the resurrection of the dead, the most important commandment. His parables were probably told here. Naturally, it was here that he drove out the merchants (Mark 11, Luke 19, Matt. 21) and here that he received the woman taken in adultery (John 8:11). Some believe it was here that he spoke the inspired words: "I am the light of the world" (John 8:12).

After the death of the master, the disciples continued with their custom of meeting in the Temple (Acts 2:46; 3:11; 5:12). Later Paul of Tarsus, visiting here, found himself overwhelmed by an excited crowd which wanted to kill him, because they suspected him of having brought a Gentile friend, Trophimus of Ephesus, into the holy enclave; freed from the Roman guards, Paul preached to the crowd from a flight of steps (Acts 21:27–40).

After the terrible events of A.D. 70 there remained on the esplanade where the Temple had stood only a pile of ruins, until Emperor Hadrian (135 on) put up an altar to Jupiter there. Following the pagan interlude, a basilica built by Constantine in the fourth century and dedicated to the Virgin seems to have stood on the site.

There were more changes at the end of the seventh century, when two grandiose Islamic buildings were erected, the Dome of the Rock and the Mosque of al-Aqsa. The first is not so much a mosque as a special shrine to cover and protect the huge piece of blond limestone on which, according to tradition, Abraham was about to sacrifice his son Isaac: an event which echoes memorably through the vaults of the sacred history of each of the three monotheistic faiths: Judaism, Christianity, and Islam.

The counterpoint is subtly evident in many other less obvious echoes. To the north of the esplanade there is a small domed edicule, known as the Kursi Issa, the "Seat of Jesus." One must not forget that the Koran too has a christology of its own, ill-conceived according to the Christian point of view but nonetheless important as evidence of the exalted position Jesus occupies in the Islamic empyrean of the great prophets. Not far from the Dome itself stands a small building whose dome is supported by pairs of slender marble columns and which is known as the Dome of the Ascension. The ascension referred to is that of Mohammed, who according to tradition prayed here before ascending from earth to heaven on the back of the legendary steed al-Buraq, and was then able to contemplate the divine presence. Some people believe that this building was put up by the Crusaders in the mistaken belief that the ascension intended is that of Christ. The misunderstanding, if true, is interesting not as something to smile about from the heights of our own superior learning, but as another reminder of the innumerable subtle links which are woven together in the context of the three faiths. Equally curious is a marble basin from a Roman temple, which has been shown to pilgrims since the Middle Ages as the "cradle of the child

Old Arab house

5

Jesus"; this tradition concerning a moment in the life of the founder of Christianity is Islamic rather than Christian.

Lastly, going just a few steps beyond the Mosque of al-Aqsa, leaving the Haram-ash-Sharif by the Moor Gate, one goes down toward the Wailing Wall. This, as everyone knows, is the most prominent remaining bit of Herod's Temple, after its destruction by the Romans. For centuries this has been a place of worship for Jews of every school and persuasion, from the strictest Orthodox to the most liberal, for their encounter with God. Because of the tragic nature of events, for many centuries this communion was a more or less desperate lament over the fate of the nation, and the wall became known as the "Wailing Wall."

All over the vast esplanade of Haram-ash-Sharif significant moments in the history of the three faiths appear linked by a secret and subtle web of connections.

Unfortunately, tradition does not prepare us to realize such things.

Ecumenism is a new concept; it leaves many people puzzled, doubtful, and disturbed. Even those who view it with sympathy see it as being contained within the sphere of the churches and sects which cause internal strife among the three religions themselves. Too many deeply rooted prejudices hound us with the idea that "the others" are "infidels," "Gentiles," "heretics." Too many highly emotive expressions ("betraying the religion of one's fathers," "abandoning one's faith," "conversion," "apostasy," etc.) crop up in our languages for real spiritual interchange to be yet possible beyond the limits of each of the three faiths.

Then of course there is ignorance to contend with. How many Christians, for instance, if they have no special education on the subject, know anything precise, detailed, or documented about the spiritual bases of Judaism or Islam? And vice versa, of course. Exclusivism is at work on all three sides of the triangle. People are born into one of the three fields, they mostly meet with biased teaching, and they remain entrenched in their positions until they die. The pernicious idea that Truth (with a capital T) is "our exclusive possession" ends by forming three virtually noncommunicating, watertight compartments within monotheist humanity. Only during the last few years have a few generous and daring bridges been put out by adventurous souls.

It is true that to arrive at real impartiality, at a true spiritual openness favorable to all three faiths, one must first put oneself outside their whole configuration. Yet the majority of modern men are in precisely this position. An attitude of agnosticism toward all religions, of vague theism, possibly accompanied by the formal observance of various practices prompted by family tradition, is a normal condition for men in the big cities of both East and West.

Now, I would like to be allowed to adopt a position which may appear unacceptable, both to the believers in the three faiths and to those who see religion as an

6

outdated phase of human evolution. If we have really "moved on from the religions of our ancestors," then this is a singularly propitious moment to look back and consider the whole religious phenomenon calmly yet with feeling, with detachment but also with warm and human involvement.

What, essentially, is religion? It is an expression of man's perennial, eternal attempt to throw a bridge between himself, between his society, and the ultimate secret of things, Mystery: between what is seen, with all its enigmas—death, suffering, injustice—and what might possibly be able to justify and explain it all.

On the whole, modern man rejects the traditional explanations, and often very shrilly too. And dare we say he is completely wrong? Mostly these explanations are the fruit of cultural, economic, and social conditions entirely different from our own, of different assessments of the truth and of its credentials, of a magical, miracle-ridden vision of the world. They are almost always grounded in heavenly revelations, which he rejects for this very reason: he finds the idea of a message from the absolute, of God's microphone, quite absurd. He is too used to thinking in another, antithetical way, to looking for the ultimate criteria of truth in experience, and to seeing something final and immutable in the law of nature.

Yet the mysteries of life and death remain absolutely and utterly unchanged: it is childish to think that, in this respect, we might be different from our remotest forebears. The disappearance of a beloved person distressed a Neanderthal man in his cave, just as it distresses a nuclear physicist in his apartment or as it will distress a spaceman in his capsule tomorrow. Modern man has no reason to become irreligious in an absolute sense, except as a momentary reaction against the spiritual slavery of outdated conceptions. The really modern man must find new forms, ways, and approaches to venerate the unseen, to cast new bridges between himself and the secret of the last things. May one dare to hope that the twenty-first century will tackle this task?

Meanwhile—even without finding a way of his own, a true expression of entirely new times and climates of thought—he is in a position to turn, open-mindedly, and assenting basically, even if not formally and in detail, toward all the attempts of the past.

For centuries Jerusalem has been sacred to three faiths, theoretically parallel, in reality often ferocious enemies; this fact makes the city incredibly complex. I believe one could safely say that no other point on the globe contains such a variety of architecture, theology, ritual, language, gastronomy, and modes of dress within so small a space. Astronomers speak of curious stars they call "white dwarfs," which are very small but of such compact matter, consisting only of single atomic nuclei, that they manage to exert a gravitational pull of incredible power. Jerusalem is a white dwarf of the spirit.

The Old City—now contained within the fine walls erected by Suleiman the

7

The Tower of David

Magnificent in about 1538—rises like an Eastern San Gimignano or Carcassonne, the sort of city that might be pictured in the hands of a patron saint in a medieval fresco, bristling with towers, domes, belfries, and minarets. The light, harmonious color of the original rock remains in the hewn stone; the sun seems to give it life, and a special light. The encircling wall is intact, with its corner towers, with its famous gates, the Damascus Gate, St. Stephen's Gate, the Jaffa Gate, the Zion Gate, and the rest. The Golden Gate, as we shall see, still stands severely closed, because legend has it that the future Messiah of the Jews is to pass through it.

The usual way into the city is through the Damascus Gate. This is a very dignified construction, in which the basic masses are enlivened a little by several machicolations, some slight decorations, and the lighthearted touch of the ornamental battlements. By the middle of the sixteenth century, Suleiman knew quite well that artillery made gates more or less useless as elements of defense; so he saw to it that this construction should be an eminently decorative and complex one. And in this he succeeded admirably.

Inside the gate, and just beyond it, the road makes two unexpected twists—originally a way of increasing security, since it afforded an opportunity to repulse any enemy who might have penetrated so far. After this the road runs straight through the whole city, along the old Cardo of the Roman Aelia Capitolina. But the Cardo has long since lost its original character. We know that during the Byzantine period, and perhaps later too, there was a colonnade, of which there are still a few traces here and there. Today the original route of the colonnade is lined by a series of *suks*—little markets in which people, dust, wares, and unexpected shafts of light mingle in a seething mass of movement, color, smell, and sound, not to mention the shifting web of unseen dealings spun between seller and buyer, customer and purveyor, browser and peddler.

The crowd is like a whirlpool, and not only of people, but of different traditions, customs, garments, faces, and skins. Before you have had a chance to admire an Orthodox priest, as pale and elegant as if he had just stepped down from an El Greco painting, he has disappeared into a crowd of fat Arab women, draped in gowns that look like carpets. Follow him under the arch of a Gothic doorway dating from the time of the Crusaders, and you are suddenly faced with a group of strictly Orthodox young Jews, dressed in their long overcoats, with their round fur caps and two fair ringlets of curly hair—*peyess*—hanging down their cheeks. Should you make a move to photograph them, they cover their faces with their hands. Here are a mullah, a rabbi, and two Franciscan friars, followed by a group of Arabs with their heads covered by large kerchiefs, the kaffiyeh, held in place by a dark circlet of goat's hair, the aqal.

Every now and again you see Israeli soldiers, men and young girls; the men look like resistance fighters, with large hats, dusty scarves, and "uzzi" guns, the locally invented variation of tommy guns; the girls are very nicely got up, somewhat in the manner of air hostesses. Then a trail of innocent if dollar-laden Americans, little old

8

Right
The Tomb of Absalom

Next two pages
Valley of Kedron

ladies with curly white hair and light flowered dresses, and cheerful boys and girls, all with their cameras.

The crowd pulls you along with it. You smell spices, incense, animal fat, gasoline, sweat, frying, dust, brilliantine, treacly sweets. Snatches of Arab song mingle with the cries of vendors, the shouts of people driving off importunate small boys. You get sucked down relentlessly into the narrower parts of the *suk*. You pass under pointed arches, past a swirling vista of little windows, gratings, towers, domes. You are harassed by an absurdly picturesque scene you would like to resist ("I know it's cheap, I know it's a postcard!") but then you feel cornered, you succumb to admiration. For instance, a blacksmith's den, black and smoky, with two huge figures hammering at an object in red-hot iron; the scene is illuminated by a ray of sun, falling perpendicularly from a hole in the roof. All goes by in a split second. Then other things to see, to hear, to sniff out, pursue, or avoid clamor for attention.

Bloody heads of goats, for instance, dripping and sinister, placed in baskets. Then milk, cheese, cream. Or vegetables, eggplants, green watermelons, luscious pumpkins. Nordic miniskirted thighs skipping by. Fruit, disemboweled lambs, rosaries, the sound of bells, children selling pens, batteries, notebooks, a shop window of souvenirs for Catholic nuns, smoke, the stench of urine, rotten fruit, burning rubber; the local beauty mincing proudly by, with the great black eyes of an Empress Theodosia or Queen Zenobia.

The variety of beings and things is only a shimmering, colored reflection of the profound variety of their invisible counterparts. Here three universes and three conceptions of life are brought face to face with one another and permeate one another. Everything varies, changes from one moment to another, everywhere homage is rendered to minuscule and particular sovereignties. Here, as a sign of respect, you must take off your hat, there you have to cram it firmly on your head; here you mustn't enter with your shoes on, there it's anathema to smoke; here pork is taboo, there blood, farther on it's fish without scales; here you *may* drink wine, there you *must* drink wine, elsewhere you're in trouble if you do! Here there is baptism, there circumcision; here the risen Messiah is celebrated, there a future Messiah is awaited; here prophets are quoted, there they hymn the Prophet. Here Friday is a holy day, there Saturday, elsewhere Sunday. Here is it 1969, there 5729, one step farther on 1389.

Here all art is allowed, sculpture and painting; there only painting; and farther on, nothing—content yourself with the arabesque and sibylline anagram. Here you may have several wives; there, only one, though you will be allowed to divorce her without difficulty; elsewhere, once you've chosen your woman, you've got her for life. Here the solar calendar predominates, there the moon is celebrated. Here bells are rung, there the shofar; farther on you can hear the voice, broadcast nowadays, of the muezzin from the top of a minaret. Here they are ascetic and Franciscan, there hedonistic and indulgent. Here traditionalist, there Reformed. Here they dress in white, there in black or beige; here they wear stars, there crosses, elsewhere crescents. And headdress, for instance, is a subtle, profound, and mysterious matter—almost as

9

Steps leading to the Wailing Wall

abstruse and esoteric as everything concerning the different ways of slaughtering animals.

So Jerusalem is a pleasant modern Babel, with its golden light and cobalt skies. I confess that when one is faced with so much fantasy in the fields of metaphysics and clothing, chronology and diet, theurgy and gastronomy, eschatology and scatology, homiletics and sex, the most insistent thought is often not very reverent: poor God, how can you hope to make any sense out of this cosmic brew of your multifarious creation?

Another important aspect of Jerusalem emerges when one knows a little of its history: we are faced with a city, not of peace—as a facile etymology of its name would have one believe—but of war.

This fact struck me at my very first visit there.

As the bus went up from Tel Aviv I noted surprising monuments. The road ran peacefully around the foothills, amid lush olive groves. The countryside was reminiscent of central Italy, of Umbria or Tuscany; there were backdrops that Giotto or Beato Angelico might have chosen for his frescoes or paintings.

Suddenly the horizon closed in on us; the road, all bends and curves, ran along the floor of a deep valley sunk between steep wooded slopes. At the roadside stood the hulks of trucks, homemade armored cars. They were as bare as the bones of camels who have died in the desert, evenly covered with a layer of bright rust; and on them were placed wreaths of withered flowers, also more or less fossilized. I turned to a neighbor for information and was told that they were the remains of vehicles whose drivers, in 1948, had tried to run the Arab blockade of Jerusalem. "Our law doesn't allow us to put up statues as monuments, so these are our monuments. They commemorate exchanges of fire, unfortunate skirmishes, and the poor devils who gave their lives in them." Quoting from one of the psalms, the stronger spirits wrote on the sides of their vehicles: "If I forget thee, O Jerusalem, let my right hand forget her cunning."

Near the Old City—it was just after the end of the Six-Day War (1967)—I found other surprising little monuments, which reminded me of the fossilized vehicles I had seen earlier along the road. These were heaps of stone, the height of a man, together with bits of armored cars and fragments of firearms, decorated with flowers and branches. There were bits of writing, too, though I could not make out anything from the arabesque of Hebrew consonants. But the date June 7th stood out clearly; people stopped, looked, and commented; mothers pointed out "the thing" to their children, who stared at it solemnly; I thought again of the words of my neighbor on the bus. These too were "monuments." While the others, lower down along the road, had been swallowed up into the questionable pomp of history, which sanctifies and distances, these were the remains of yesterday; they had all the horror of the current news item, of recent death, of things which are "still happening."

10

Right
Benei Hazir, Jewish tomb

Next eight pages
The Wailing Wall

Suddenly, there was the old Jerusalem. Now it is completely surrounded by fine paved roads and parks are being made below the walls, but then the traces of the war were still alarmingly vivid. There were houses shattered by explosions, others roofless or with the protruding remains of broken beams and rafters. Windows gaped open on the sky; for a moment the peerless blue distracted the eye from the scenes of violence and destruction. Some rooms, gutted, still bore signs of fire; black tongues on the wall showed how the flames had leapt upward.

Bulldozers were working feverishly, raising a thick white dust that swirled in the wind. They were moving mounds of masonry, knocking down the last remaining bits of wall still standing; they were gathering together girders, heaps of twisted iron, bent and positively knotted together, like *tagliatelle,* a meal for giants with metal teeth. Farther on, leaning against a bit of old masonry, stood the hulk of a bus riddled with bullet holes, devoured by the flames that had stripped and roasted it; all that was left was its black iron skeleton.

I saw old Jerusalem with its towers, surrounded by walls and barbicans, machicolations and battlements. The walls I saw were those of Suleiman the Magnificent, but previously there had been those of Saladin, the Crusaders, the Byzantines, the Romans, Nehemiah, David and the Jebusites, down through the centuries to an ever smaller and older nucleus. And that nucleus had always been a fortress, a point to be defended or taken by storm. Jerusalem is a whole array of military buildings, solidly set in the chronicles of martial deeds, in the three-thousand-year-old succession of warring sovereignties.

I don't know why I had imagined Jerusalem as being so different. How does one actually imagine a "holy city"? I wonder. I had imagined domes, porticoes, cloisters, bell towers, mosques, a grassy tree-filled open space, technicolor travelogue, in fact boring, where few things happen, and those few neatly anticipated; it would be crossed by monkish figures, lean black-clothed men deep in sublime thought, the air would be filled with psalms and prayers and the occasional chime of bells, and be heavy with the scent of incense.

The reality was a shock. Here was Jerusalem: an eternal battlefield. Everything was interesting, genuine, compact, warm, alive; terrible and cruel. A popular song has a verse about "Jerusalem of gold and copper and light." But a simple soldier, Meir Ariel, more alive to the realities of the moment, rephrased this verse: "Jerusalem of iron and lead and blood."

Of blood! Anyone with some familiarity with the history of Jerusalem throughout the centuries can thank the gods for one thing only: that blood isn't indelible, that it melts away with the rain, dries in the sun and disappears. If blood were indelible, Jerusalem would be red, all red.

After the first sense of surprise, going through the curtain of great walls, you find yourself among the famous shrines; the holy places of the Jews, the Christians, the

11

followers of Islam. And here you suddenly realize that Jerusalem is a city of the sword and of fire, of blood and tears, precisely *because* it is the city of the star, the cross, and the crescent.

A recent mammoth publication, *Cities of Destiny,* which gives a supersonic review of thirty centuries of history and forty thousand leagues of the planet earth, with chapters on Athens, Rome, Alexandria, Ch'ang-an, Constantinople, Florence, Venice, Delhi, Mexico City, St. Petersburg, Vienna, Paris, London, New York, had no chapter on Jerusalem. This struck me as being like publishing a book on astronomy without mentioning the sun, or on pathology without mentioning cancer. Whether one considers it as sun or cancer, light of the faiths, beacon of Moses, Christ, Mohammed, or sore caused by the fanaticisms that have torn and indeed are still tearing it, if in fact there is a city of destiny on our tormented globe, then that city is Jerusalem. A city which no one can avoid, of which all others are more or less suburbs.... The things that have been thought, said, and sung in Jerusalem, the things that have happened, been perpetrated, and suffered in Jerusalem continually concern a large part of mankind. If history is basically a travail of ideas, Jerusalem is one of the most productive mothers of the many ideas that have made and continue to make history. Certainly Rome was stronger, more splendid than Jerusalem, Babylon knew greater luxury, London and New York are infinitely bigger and richer, Paris may be more learned, Florence more sophisticated, Vienna gayer, but all had or have limits to their *floruit,* they were and are not, or were not and are. Jerusalem, accursed or holy as one pleases, has existed for three thousand years, truly marked by destiny, herself immortal dealer of destinies.

When a great, powerful, and civilized modern country plans a mad policy of hatred and then of annihilation, killing millions of men, women, and children with dizzying scientific efficiency, the root cause, in the last analysis, is Jerusalem. When a whole continent, South America, languishes on the brink of revolution because of blatant economic and social inequalities, because of a wealthy class closely linked to a backward-looking and short-sighted clergy, it all leads back to Jerusalem. Hundreds of millions of Catholics make a case of conscience out of birth control. Jerusalem. Is the Middle East a powder magazine in continual danger of explosion? Jerusalem. Are India and Pakistan divided over Kashmir? Yes, Islam, Mohammed, but always, in the last analysis, Jerusalem, mother of monotheisms. No divorce in Italy? Jerusalem again.

And if—as has been done many times—one regards Communism as the supreme Christian heresy, then there is almost nothing of any importance happening in the world today that cannot finally be traced back to Jerusalem. Half a century of Communist rule in Moscow, the war in Vietnam, the Peking polemic, Tito and Castro— the influence of Jerusalem no longer has any limits of latitude and longitude. It is not too far-fetched to see subtle links between Communism and Christianity. The two may confront one another as mortal enemies, but they are still thesis and antithesis of a broader historical dialectic. On a philosophical level it is legitimate to emphasize how far a thesis and its antithesis, while acting as opposing poles of the forces that mold future development, mutually condition and influence one another. But it is in less general, more specific circumstances that such connections are seen at their clearest. From trivial facts—Marx the son of a converted Jew and therefore the heir to a strong ethical and religious family tradition—to the essential spirit of Christianity as it emerged at the beginning, as a movement of the humble and oppressed, of the slaves, at first in messianic expectation of the kingdom of God and then, after the failure of Parousia, intent on reinterpreting the message and on setting up the kingdom of God in history. In this sense we may say that Marx, and Engels, were great reformers, descendants of Luther, Zwingli, and Calvin.

Having become heirs to empires or living in symbiosis with empires, the Churches had long forgotten to act on what might be considered essential parts of the original message—everything pertaining to the brotherhood of man, to charity understood not as a palliative but as total redemption. That Marx and Engels should have placed themselves in firm antithesis to religion as they knew it ("opium of the people") was quite natural; every real reformer bulldozes and destroys in order to transcend. It is also quite natural that they should have talked the scientific and philosophical language of their time. But there is something in the impetus of their great work, a hidden spring which was not mere erudition but implied love for suffering humanity and indignation at the conditions of this suffering, forces which had their roots somewhere deep down in the complex totality of our spiritual inheritance. If this were not the case, the image of the German scholar, with his wild hair and chaotic appearance, often pustulous and flatulent, who sat for years at his desk in the British Museum accumulating information like the drip making the stalagmite, leafing through texts and filling files that were to shatter the world, would be fascinating but completely remote.

Now, if Marx had worked in the public libraries of Tokyo or Calcutta one would turn to Buddha or Krishna to trace the roots of his indignation. But the British Museum is in the heart of London; we can think only of Christ, Amos, Habakkuk, Isaiah, St. Francis; and so, once again, of Jerusalem.

There is less distance between *Das Kapital* and Revelation than one might imagine. The first speaks the language of science, the second that of mysticism; both are voices of men projecting a dream of justice into the future. Both have their roots sunk in a land called Jerusalem.

Jerusalem wears its cosmic destiny lightly, elegantly, even with humor.

Let us go to the Holy Sepulcher. For a moment, let us forget about religion, about sacred history, reminders of the central drama of a faith that has nourished much of the world for thousands of years. Let us also set aside all aesthetic considerations. Let us say only that, if the Jews have to make do with a ruin for their most jealously guarded rites, the Christians have to put a good face on one of the oddest topographical, architectural, historical, and stylistic hodgepodges on the face of the globe.

Without looking around, let us go straight to the center of the building, to the great nave, now the property of the Greeks, in the heart of the Katholikon, beneath the high dome through which filters an even, respectful light, like that at the bottom of the sea. There, in the center of a floor of much-worn polychrome marble, like an old piece of well-darned cloth, stands a square stone, the size of a cushion, with a little circular hollow in the center. Near it is a brass lampstand, fitted out to hold small candles. Then there is also an odd red stone affair (said to be "stone from the Mount of Olives") similar to an ornamental garden urn, plump and firm as a fruit; an object for which, if you came across it in a junkshop, you would try in vain to find a use, a meaning, a purpose.

Well, what is it? It is the world's navel.

When, in 1967, I visited the place for the first time, I found myself amid streams of people of all nationalities. I caught snatches of their comments, hunks of German verbs *(darf, mussten, geworden)*, puffs of French adjectives *(lumineux, sensationnel, risible)*, little rushes of Anglo-Saxon monosyllables *(now stop that)*, and unknown phonetic burblings: Indo-European babblings, Semitic babblings, Ural-Altaic babblings. A French group arrived, led by a guide, plainly highly cultured, who was pointing out to them, in the language of an academician and the pitch of a Russian bass, the more recondite historical details of this memory-riddled spot. He was quoting Ezekiel fluently: "... the people that are gathered out of the nations, which have gotten cattle and goods, that dwell in the midst of the land" (Ezek. 38:12). So for at least twenty-five centuries this place had served as the world's navel.

There is no knowing whether the learned guide knew that two other points in Jerusalem contest its umbilical honors; oddly enough, one of them is the Damascus Gate. But this is a minor detail. The essential fact is that for thousands of years Jerusalem has been regarded as the world's center. In the sixth century A.D. the Egyptian merchant and traveler, and later monk, Cosmas Indicopleustes, thought of abandoning the Greek idea of a spherical earth, considering it incompatible with divine revelation, and arranged the known lands into a map in the form of a rectangle with Jerusalem at the center. A similar conception was dominant in Western culture until the beginnings of humanism and the period of the great geographical discoveries, when it became untenable. One of the most beautiful maps with Jerusalem in the center was drawn by Richard Haldingham in about 1280, and is now in Hereford Cathedral.

This sense of Jerusalem's centrality in space and time was gradually refined, like gold filigree. Not only did heaven and earth meet here in the drama of the Incarnation, Redemption, and Resurrection, but the blood of Christ, dripping from the cross, is said to have fallen on the skull of Adam, who was buried beneath those stones. Other legends flourished, were embroidered upon, perfected. Adam was said to have brought with him into the world a branch of the tree of good and evil. This

14

everlasting wood, kept in Jerusalem, caused the Queen of Sheba to have strange visions—so much so that Solomon had it buried. Mysteriously, it reappeared on the surface of the pool of Bethesda. It was there that Christ's murderers went to get the wood to make his cross. So that, if on the one hand the blood of the Redeemer fell to bathe, and baptize, the skull of the first sinner, on the other hand the tree of error served as an instrument of expiation. A complete and perfect circle!

All this is very significant. Every great civilization of the past has chosen its own world center in time and space. For some—Egypt—it was linear (the Nile); for others—India, for instance—it was an immense phallic pillar, Mount Meru, the Great Himalaya, the true hinge of the universe. At Angkor Thom, in Cambodia, Mount Meru was represented by the central pinnacle of the gigantic Bayon: its axis continued underground down to a well, and the central cell, forbidden to the public, was occupied, on certain astronomic recurrences, by the king, who, by taking his place at the center of the cosmos, was identified with the divinity.

All this is the collective age-old expression of one of man's basic needs: to make himself a home in the universe. Here we are, mysteriously surrounded by emptiness, darkness, death: what sense has it all? Where are the high, the low, the door, the hand, the eye, the why? The universe does not exist as such; all that does exist are interpretations of it. The human condition was the same in the year 100,000 B.C. as it will be in A.D. 100,000. Why are we born? Why do we die? What sense have evil, pain, suffering—particularly when they fall upon the just or children, or those who are blameless, poor, bewildered animals? Has existence any purpose? Are we curious beings standing on the edge of the void, or hollow little creatures at the foot of an impregnable fortress? Are we an episode, a step, a link, a wave of something that transcends us? Shall we ever know?

The fact that we are familiar with the atoms and their secrets, that we can transplant hearts or leap off toward distant planets, measure galaxies, play with light-years as though they were confetti, does not alter the situation in the slightest; indeed, the more man knows, the more mysterious the final things appear, as though they were shielded by the need for a qualitative leap in understanding. The fortunate barbarian could believe that his gods, or his tribal chief, explained destinies, beginnings, ends; but we have burst all the balloons and they won't fly any more; the empty remains have fallen to the ground at our feet.

Man and mystery: these are the two terms, possibly irreducible, of all conscious existence. The mystery is stupendous and fearful, like a star-filled winter sky seen from the top of a mountain; man considers it for a moment, in fascination but also in anguish, then seeks for safety in the welcoming warmth of some more human haven. A real civilization, mature and perfected, is indeed one which offers man an organic interpretation of the mystery; it offers him a habitable universe. Every civilization provides him with origins and a history, it organizes sky and earth, the Cause and causes, love and death, good and evil; it acts as his compass, his parent, his buffer, bumper, anchor, gives him air to breathe and eyes to see with; it acts as

15

Steps leading to the Tomb of the Kings

stimulant or sedative, as occasion demands. It gives him a theology and a census, a calendar, physics, ethics, art, and sometimes (Rome, China) even an empire that coincides, or nearly, with the ecumene.

In the Christian universe Jerusalem was projected from the earth beyond the starry heights, and came down again, idealized, as the capital of the kingdom of God. "And I... saw the holy city, new Jerusalem, coming down from God out of heaven, prepared as a bride adorned for her husband" (Rev. 21:2). "And [it] had a wall great and high, and had twelve gates, and at the gates twelve angels, and names written thereon, which are the names of the twelve tribes of the children of Israel. On the east three gates; on the north three gates; on the south three gates; and on the west three gates. And the wall of the city had twelve foundations, and in them the names of the twelve apostles of the Lamb.... And the city lieth foursquare, and the length is as large as the breadth... twelve thousand furlongs.... And the building of the wall... was of jasper; and the city was pure gold, like unto clear glass. And the foundations of the wall of the city were garnished with all manner of precious stones. The first foundation was jasper; the second, sapphire; the third, a chalcedony; the fourth, an emerald. The fifth, sardonyx; the sixth, sardius; the seventh, chrysolite; the eighth, beryl; the ninth, a topaz; the tenth, a chrysoprase; the eleventh, a jacinth; the twelfth, an amethyst. And the twelve gates were twelve pearls; every several gate was of one pearl; and the street of the city was pure gold, as it were transparent glass. And I saw no temple therein; for the Lord God Almighty and the Lamb are the temple of it. And the city has no need of the sun, neither of the moon, to shine in it; for the glory of God did lighten it, and the Lamb is the light thereof" (Rev. 21:12–23).

These are luscious baroque fantasies worthy of some town-planning Fabergé who, instead of making enameled eggs for Tsarinas or little thrones of precious stones for Prussian kings, might have set about conceiving fortresses, palaces, and temples, arches, portals, and squares. In a far more spiritual sense such dreams were taken up by St. Augustine. Rome had fallen into the hands of Alaric (410) and the pagans were saying: See what happens if you repudiate the gods of your fathers for the Son of the Father! Not at all, replied Augustine: throughout the ages Rome has always been protected by her virtues, not by her gods. When her virtues failed, Rome became weak. Rome represents the *civitas terrena,* in which egoistic love, instead of love for God, finally and fatally prevailed. The contrast to Rome was Jerusalem: a symbolic and apocalyptic Jerusalem, the *civitas Dei.*

In the framework of such conceptions, which organize the mystery of life for man, a navel of the world is something very definite and altogether necessary; it may be defined as a small and much-needed seal of the cosmic order. And here one might note an interesting fact: our modern universe is probably the first in history without a center, without a line or pillar, without absolute co-ordinates.

And therefore the first universe without a navel.

16

The Tomb of the Kings, water ducts

II | ELEVEN ROWS OF STONES

Herod the Great did things wholeheartedly. All the remaining buildings of his time are not only grandiose in their general conception, they are also formidable works of engineering. The Temple of Jerusalem, destroyed by the Romans in A.D. 70, must have been one of the most impressive monuments in a period when impressive monuments were found in hundreds in all Mediterranean countries.

The most outstanding direct evidence of this work is a stretch of wall, which was part of the outer curtain in the complex of Temple buildings. Today it bounds part of the Haram-ash-Sharif to the southwest. It consists of a series of eleven rows of colossal stones, cut and dressed with extreme care, and topped by a more recent length of lighter wall. Apparently the masonry continues underground, still formed of impressively large blocks, for another seventeen yards or so; it has simply been buried by the centuries-old deposit of debris and rubble. (The Archaeological Expedition of the Hebrew University excavated in 1968, after my visits to Jerusalem, some ten yards of the Haram's south wall below modern ground level, and laid bare a beautiful Herodian pavement.)

For centuries this wall was almost overwhelmed by other neighboring buildings; it could be approached only along a tiny alley. In June 1967 all the little houses that stood in front of the old ruin were destroyed; today the wall is more or less fully exposed and looks onto a small square which is itself to be restored in the near future.

Immediately after the destruction of the Temple by the Romans, the Jews who had remained in Jerusalem gathered along this bit of wall to lament the misfortunes of their country. With the passing of time this lament, this desperate meditation on the misfortunes of the race, developed into a ritual and became an act of true devotion, very important within the complex of Jewish religious feeling. For some time, it is assumed, the "wailing" also took place at the main gates of the "Noble Sanctuary," and even inside, especially in the early Moslem era, but from the Crusades to the nineteenth century non-Moslems were strictly forbidden to enter the Haram-ash-Sharif, and most Orthodox Jews even now refrain from going there, lest they tread on the Holy of Holies, reserved to the High Priest on the Day of Atonement of old—and of the messianic future, when the Temple will be rebuilt by God's own miracle. And so the remains of the Temple of Herod the Great became the "Wailing Wall" par excellence.

When I visited this famous and impressive stretch of wall for the first time in 1967, bulldozers were still leveling the ground with an ear-splitting din, moving

The Tomb of Herod's Family

stones, bits of plaster, lumps of earth, raising whirlwinds of light white dust that the wind scattered into the blue air like snow whirled by a south wind.

There was a general feeling of youthful enthusiasm. Pilgrims were arriving in the new "Jerusalem delivered" from all parts of the world to touch the wall, this lonely remnant of a vanished Temple, which is nonetheless the most sacred symbol of Jewish unity in the world.

Now, one year later, the place was better cared for, although one still felt that it was a temporary affair, that any definitive arrangement would have to be more organic, perhaps more impressive. The sun beat down fiercely. Among the gigantic stones of the wall weeds were growing—I thought I saw some caper bushes—and above it stretched an implacable blue. The Orthodox Jews seemed unaware of it. Wearing their long black overcoats and broad-brimmed hats, their curls hanging down their cheeks, they moved about alone or in groups, meditating, talking, reciting prayers.

At the foot of the wall a solid line of the faithful were standing praying, their faces turned toward the stone. The most pious were reading, reciting, their whole bodies swaying in rhythmic bowings, a sort of dance that varied from person to person. It would be easy enough to make fun of them. But the manifestations of faith are often odd, incomprehensible to people looking at them from the outside. I shall always remember how a Japanese friend defined Italy: "Oh yes, the country where you dress up twelve-year-old girls as brides and take them to eat God for the first time." I was told that one doesn't pray only with one's mouth, nor think the prayer in one's mind, but that it must be an act that is performed even by the body's most hidden cells, interpreting literally Psalm 35:10: "All my bones shall say, O Lord, who is like unto thee?" This was the reason for the movements, the rhythmical leaping, that looked like a dance.

Today I went back to visit the wall. It was a special day: the celebration of *tish' a b' av* (the ninth day of the month of Av, coinciding with July or August), an occasion commemorating the destruction of the Temple: the Babylonian one of 587 B.C. and the Roman one of A.D. 70, as well as the fall of Bethar, the last stronghold of Bar Kochba in the rebellion against the Roman Emperor Hadrian in A.D. 135. (An additional major catastrophe in Jewish history, the expulsion from Spain in 1492, occurred on this ominous date, on which also World War I broke out, according to the Jewish calendar.)

In theory it is a day of mourning. I was told that the strictest Orthodox do not wash themselves, eat no meat, read the Lamentations of Jeremiah from the day of the new moon until the ninth of the lunar month of Av (a day of complete abstinence from food). In the past, apparently, the devout used to sleep with a stone instead of a pillow, as an act of penance. In religious schools, during the same period, masters told their pupils tales of the terrible days in the past, when heroes defended the Temple in vain before surrendering it, with their lives, to the enemy. Curious transformations took place. For some obscure reason, Nero became a staunch friend of

18

Roman inscription of the Tenth Legion

the Jews; it is said that he abandoned one of his armies near Jerusalem, fleeing and becoming converted to Judaism. Indeed, a great master, Rabbi Meir, was said to be a descendant of his. The arch-scoundrel, on the other hand, was Titus, whose ideal antithesis was the national hero Bar Kochba. Only those able to uproot cedars of Lebanon with their bare hands were considered worthy of following him and fighting in his company.

Yet, curiously enough, today I was the witness of a joyful celebration, noisy and spontaneous, almost like a carnival. There were thousands of people in the square, at the foot of the wall, lit by army searchlights. Groups of the faithful were laying mats on the ground and crouching down on them to read the holy scriptures, to recite famous passages by heart, but all with a great deal of noise and gaiety, as though this were some sort of *fête champêtre,* a lunar night devoted to fertility, to gratitude for a good harvest. Rows of young people joined hands in a circle, fifty or sixty at a time, moving around with rhythmic steps, singing an Eastern melody both gentle and warlike.

I asked a young man to explain to me how this mournful occasion could have developed into an affair that seemed to be so gay.... But it is gay! he said. Now we are free. The past no longer counts. What do we say when we make a toast? *Lekhaim.* "To life!" So to life, it's the future that counts.

I saw him again a moment later, part of a group singing and dancing in a circle moving more wildly than anyone else; their dance was similar to a Greek sirtaki.

Almost all the externals of religion are strange, seen from outside. Catholics are odd as they murmur obscure sins into the shadows of an ornate tumbril, Buddhists are odd as they pray in solemn chorus for the souls of frogs or bullocks, Hindus are very strange indeed as they ecstatically follow a sadhu who mortifies his flesh with large pins or spikes, Shintoists are odd as they dance drunkenly, carrying their gods on a palanquin amid the cars, buses, elevated railways, and skyscrapers of the world's greatest metropolis, the Parsis are odd, leaving the dead to the starving vultures.... One has to see things from within to understand; only history takes us inside them; the history of facts and the history of ideas. Only history can lead us to a point where everything becomes clear, where we can say: If I had been in their place I would be doing it too.

Why should a completely modern crowd dance at the foot of an old wall, on a moonlit evening, as coolness spreads over the hills of Judaea? What was the origin of this special relationship between man and stone? Between Man and Wall?

19

Turkish tower

III | THE CITY OF MELCHIZEDEK

Jerusalem upon two hills is seen,
Of height unequal, and turned face to face;
A valley interposing sinks between,
And marks them from each other by its trace.

(TASSO)

Jerusalem stands on a part of the mountains of Judaea that has, for various reasons, been occupied by man since earliest times. This point stands at the junction between two important trade routes and has the extraordinary advantage of linking a perennial spring (Gihon) and a promontory excellently suited to fortification.

With regard to the trade routes, a glance at the map of Palestine will show that, precisely at the level of Jerusalem, the main north–south route following the crests of the rounded hills of Samaria and Judaea crosses one of the east–west routes, putting the valley of Jordan in communication with the coastal plains of the Mediterranean. Other similar points produced the cities of Shechem (then Neapolis, today Nablus) and Hebron, to the south and north of Jerusalem respectively.

Since the mountains of Judaea are not very steep and are all fairly accessible, the meeting of the two roads could have occurred at many points in the area; Jerusalem stands where it does because here a spring and a promontory were very close to each other. The promontory was easily defended, and water guaranteed the possibility of defense.

Let us look more closely at the topography, bearing in mind that today the original shape of the ground is to be imagined rather than actually seen, since over thirty centuries of intense human life on these hills have gradually flattened considerable ups and downs under piles of rubble. In ancient times there were three valleys: the valley of Kedron (or Josaphat), the valley of the Tyropoeon (now mainly in the heart of old Jerusalem and filled with debris), and the valley of Hinnom (Gehenna). Between the valleys of Kedron and the Tyropoeon there rose the spur known as Ophel, the site of the earliest settlement.

These earliest settlements certainly date back very far in time, probably to the beginnings of the bronze age, the third millennium B.C.

In 1926 a curious terra-cotta statuette was discovered in Egypt, its limbs mutilated and bearing an inscribed execration. Experts have dated it between 2000 and 1900 B.C. What is the story behind it? At that time the greatest power in the eastern Mediterranean was Egypt, whose sway extended along the coasts of Palestine and into the lands of Canaan (later to be conquered by the Israelites) in the form of a pro-

Lane, Jewish quarter,
Old City

tectorate. The region, mainly mountainous and therefore unsuited to being administered directly, was subdivided into numerous city-states and small kingdoms. When a vassal was misbehaving, failing in his duty toward the Egyptian sovereign, or neglecting to pay his tribute on time, he was intimidated with a harsh rebuke by magic, which may make one smile today but which then, within the framework of primitive thought and because of the charismatic aura emanating from the figure of the Pharaoh, could be very effective. A portrait of the offending "king" would be covered with inscribed curses and then the statuette would be mutilated and buried. This was a rite known as "execration."

It so happens that on one of these statuettes, the one discovered in Egypt, there appears a name which experts read as (U)rushalimum, that is, Jerusalem. This was still in very remote times, during the bronze age (about 1900 B.C.).

This name has been interpreted in a variety of ways. Some scholars, for instance, derive it from Yeru and Shalem, giving it the sense of "city founded by Shalem." Shalem was apparently the name of a divinity whose cult was fairly widespread among western Semites, particularly the Amorites. Evidently the word *shalem* can be considered the same as the modern *shalom,* or peace. It should be remembered that the Amorites were close relatives of the Hebrews: "thy father was an Amorite, and thy mother an Hittite" (Ezek. 16:3).

For centuries people have been forwarding hypotheses about the origin of the name Jerusalem. The Talmud gives the following mythological explanation: "Abraham called the city Jeru [revered fear] and Shem, son of Noah, called it salem [peace]. The Lord God said: 'If I call it Jeru, as Abraham did, then Shem, a just man, will be offended, and if I call it Shalem, as Shem did, then Abraham, a just man, will be offended. So I shall call it both—Jerusalem.'" Such an explanation obviously is interesting only in so far as it reveals something of the thought and mode of reasoning of those men who composed an ancient and revered religious document.

Another reference to Urusalim is found, in cuneiform, on some of the clay tablets composing the archive of Pharaoh Amenophis (1377–1358 B.C.) which were discovered at Tel el-Amarna in 1887. This was a letter from Abdi-Hipa, king of Urusalim, in which he asked for the Pharaoh's help because his own territory was being overrun by rebels he could not subdue.

"I fall seven times at the feet of my Lord.... A city in the land of Jerusalem, Beit Lahmi, a city of the king's, has passed over to the people of Keilah ... let my king heed Abdi-Hipa his servant, and send him archers to reconquer the royal territory for the king...."

As early as Genesis, in connection with Abraham, we find a passage which many people regard as a reference to Jerusalem. In Chapter 14 there is talk of a "war" fought near the Dead Sea, during which the cities of Sodom and Gomorrah were despoiled of many goods and of their possessions by a coalition of four "kings." Just at that time Lot, Abraham's nephew, was living in Sodom. Hearing of the war, Abraham immediately set out with 318 servants, drove the robber "kings" beyond Damascus,

21

House, Jewish quarter,
Old City

and gallantly regained nephew, goods, women, and servants. On his return Abraham was greeted and congratulated not only by the king of Sodom but by a certain Melchizedek, identified only as "king of Salem" and as "priest of the All Highest," who offered him bread and wine and blessed the victor. Abraham paid him a tithe, then went back to his nomadic wanderings through the steppes and deserts.

It is worth pausing for a moment to consider this somewhat mysterious incident. It brings us right into what one might call "the Jerusalem atmosphere," a world where the earth is subtly (but also unexpectedly) transformed by the influence of visions and epiphanies, where the great marble vaults of the *hekhal* (palace of God) or the *merkabah* (chariot of the All Highest) may seem more real than a mud hovel or a caravan standing in front of our very eyes. Somehow it is not like Ireland, where myths and legends hang at ground level, like a mist from the branches of the woodland trees, producing *hiraeth* in the soul, a feeling of great sadness and yearning. That is not the way it is in Jerusalem: myths, dreams, visions come down to earth like reflections from a terrible gleaming metallic sky, they sweep along men and their passions, things, history, producing blood, fire, iron, stones, flesh, howlings, creatures, children, tents, and deserts in a relentless flux.

To return to the Melchizedek incident, the reader who sees Genesis as a simple story will find here only a picturesque episode lost in the mists of time, which took place in the lands smitten by the sun of Coelesyria, involving four robber kings and a sheik who knew how to make himself respected.

But a critical eye will be caught by many points that are exegetically tough. It is quite clear that the whole of Chapter 14, as scholars have pointed out, "shows no connection in either form or content with the rest of Genesis." The more iconoclastic regard the whole chapter as a later interpolation, a midrash, that is, an example of that "type of Judaic literature, which developed especially after the exile, in which historical facts were re-elaborated or completely invented in order to exalt certain characters or to inculcate certain religious or moral precepts." Clearly, they say, what we have here is a glorification of Abraham, an attempt to hallow the payment of the tithes to the priests of Jerusalem. The more cautious use the strange names of the kings to try to trace links with the historical facts of the time (nineteenth century B. C.?) and not entirely without success, it must be said. The few ascertainable points of correspondence do in fact suggest a variety of solutions. So the war of words continues, and seems unlikely to abate.

Parallel with the analyses of the exegetes—indeed, since much earlier times— the keen-eyed faithful have read an extraordinary wealth of hints and messages into this episode. The mysterious Melchizedek, king of Salem, priest of El-Elyon, to be identified with the All Highest, the Lord (see Psalm 110), appears out of the blue, without either ancestors or descendants. Who was this Melchizedek, whose Hebrew name means "king of righteousness"? Why did Abraham pay him the tithe, recognizing him as a superior? Minds begin to whir, thoughts gallop. Is it not odd that he should be king *and* "priest of the All Highest" precisely in that city where, a thousand

22

years later, there were to be kings and priests of the true God? Might it not be some sort of sign? Might it not be a symbolical, exemplary exchange in the great dialogue between God and man, between heaven and earth? Psalm 110 shows us the invisible building, with its age-old associations, already established. In this psalm Jehovah addresses the Messiah and says: "Thou art a priest for ever after the order of Melchizedek." The ancient king of Salem was therefore considered as a precursor of the Messiah, his perfect paradigm.

The king-priests of the Maccabees, too, in particular John Hyrcanus, referred back to Melchizedek when they assumed the double power of king and priest, without having the hereditary rights of the Zadokite descendants of the order of Aaron.

But this is only the beginning. Biblical themes, like musical motifs in the great works of Bach, appear, disappear, and reappear in varying yet recognizable filigree, mingle with other cascades of sound, with crystalline flowerings, moving upward toward pinnacles of irresistible splendor. St. Paul takes up the theme of Melchizedek: he stresses that he is the "king of justice" (which is what his name means in the language of Canaan), the king of peace *(salem,* today's Hebrew *shalom* and Arabic *salam)*, and he stresses particularly that he has "no father, nor mother, nor ancestors, that his life has no beginning nor end." Melchizedek therefore prefigures the priestship of Christ; in fact, he is someone who stands outside time, an "eternal priest."

The figure of the Messiah in Hebrew thought, particularly in the late Hellenistic period, is very complex: at one extreme there was the dream of the militant leader who would free Israel from the rule of the *kittim* (Romans), and he was the Davidic, royal Messiah; at the other was the spiritual saviour, who was to bring about the new order in men's hearts, the Messiah prefigured in the prophecies of the Deutero-Isaiah about the "servant of the Lord." Now St. Paul, especially with regard to the Jews, had the extremely difficult task of showing that Jesus combined in his person the quality of the royal Messiah, in that he was a descendant of David, with those of the spiritual Messiah, in so far as he was son of God. Jesus belonged to the tribe of Judah, therefore in theory he was excluded from the supreme priesthood of the spiritual Messiah, reserved since the time of Moses for Levites. Paul, with the persuasiveness of a great and ingenious orator, resolved the difficulty brilliantly in the Epistle to the Hebrews. Jesus, he says, is the Messiah; of the Messiah it has been said (Psalm 110) that he shall be a priest for ever after the order of Melchizedek, so that Jesus is relinked to Melchizedek, whose rights he inherits, "abolishing the earlier prescription" requiring that he should belong to the tribe of Levi.

The Church Fathers raised complex new spires on this cathedral: the bread and wine which Melchizedek offered Abraham became an image of the Eucharist, whose sacrifice they foreshadowed. Finally the supreme pinnacle: various Fathers have supported the view that Melchizedek was a living manifestation of the son of God in person, and therefore a proto-Christ. His existence would have produced a crypto-, archaeo-Parousia.

Stairway, Moslem quarter,
Old City

This is all "pure Jerusalem." The exhilarating city has worked its exquisite gnostic miracle. The recitation of abstruse facts about robber-kings and patriarchs of thirty-eight centuries ago has gradually become something richer, has been transmuted, has soared from the world of matter through the aeons of dreams and consciousness to the realm of cosmic epiphanies. Past, future, world history, the Pleroma, the En-soph, the Absolute and its mysterious presence among men, all are involved.

But there is another very important link between Abraham and Jerusalem, one of the many that stress the holy character of the city for the three great monotheistic faiths. Beneath the cupola of the Dome of the Rock, built about 691 by Abul-Miqdam Ridja—a place held in great veneration by the Moslems—there is a huge irregular stone, goldish in color, pock-marked, and as old as the world. On this stone, according to tradition, Abraham made Isaac kneel; it was there that the patriarch then raised his weapon to kill his son as an offering for Jehovah, and it was there that, at the last moment, an angel appeared to stay the father's hand ("Lay not thine hand upon the lad, neither do anything unto him: for now I know that thou fearest God, seeing thou hast not withheld thy son, thine only son from me" [Gen. 22:12]).

Later, on this same rock, it is said, stood the Holy of Holies (debir) of Solomon's great Temple of Jerusalem, which was finally destroyed by Titus in A.D. 70. During the Byzantine centuries a Christian church seems to have existed nearby. In the seventh century the Dome of the Rock was built, one of the most important holy places for Islam. At no other place in the world are the three monotheist faiths so close, bound together by a memory that bears witness to all of their shared spiritual descent from the patriarch Abraham.

At about what time did Abraham walk along those mountain ways? Until a few decades ago, rationalists considered Abraham a myth, a fable, a character invented to act as a common progenitor for the tribes of the Hebrews. For believers, on the other hand, every moment, every word of the Biblical story was unassailably historical. Now the age-old dialectic has produced a *rapprochement* between the two fronts, a synthesis. It is true that no archaeological facts confirm the truth of the character of Abraham and his wanderings *ab externo,* but it is thought to be very probable that his journey from Mesopotamia to the borders of Egypt does generally follow the movements of a group of nomads headed by a charismatic leader of extraordinary personality, energy, and wisdom. Such movements might have taken place about 1850 B.C. while the Middle Empire was flowering in Egypt and the first Babylonian civilization was maturing under the great Emperor Hammurabi.

How could Jerusalem have been in those remote times, before the Israelite conquest? The land of Canaan—which corresponded roughly to present-day Palestine—was not then united under one single ruler, if we discount the vague and distant Egyptian sovereignty. It was a constellation of city-states of varying degrees of size, strength, and importance. The general circumstances resembled those of pre-Macedonian Greece or, more closely still, those of Italy at the time of the communes, when the sovereignty of the Emperor was, with rare exceptions, a less tangible reality than

24

the effective one of the single communes. Toynbee calls the civilization of Canaan the "sister" of the Greek: a minor (though older) sister, of course, because the Canaanite states were fewer in number, poorer, and more provincial than their "opposite numbers" in the islands and peninsulas of Greece.

Pillar at the Gate of the Chain,
Old City

IV | FROM WILDERNESS TO PROMISED LAND

Palestine is situated across a more or less obligatory route between Mesopotamia and Egypt. Mesopotamia and Egypt are countries of plainland, vast, fertile, and therefore natural seats of empires; Palestine is small and narrow, mainly mountainous, and therefore little suited to serving as the center of a great realm. Fate has linked the history of Palestine to the destinies of Mesopotamia and Egypt. Only when the empires of the two great adjacent river basins have been in periods of crisis has Palestine been able to enjoy any degree of independence. A third element, at least during certain periods, must be added to the age-old juggling between Mesopotamia and Egypt: Anatolia. It was from Anatolia that, in ancient times, the Hittites exerted their power and, in more recent times, the Turks. Less regular, but often no less significant, were the forces of opposition or of dominion coming from the sea (Philistines, Crusaders) or the south (Arabs).

At the dawn of history Palestine (the land of the Amurru) appears as the farthest border of the Akkadian kingdom of Sargon (about 2350–2300 B.C.). It was then that cuneiform writing spread from the Persian Gulf to the Mediterranean. Later Egypt reaffirmed its rule, which lasted almost a thousand years and was interrupted only by the period (itself considerable) of the incursions of the Hyksos.

Who exactly these Shepherd Kings (or "foreigners") were is not known. From the earliest times, according to Flavius Josephus, it was thought they might be the Hebrews themselves, but today such a hypothesis seems unlikely. If it is true that the Hyksos introduced horses and war chariots into the Middle East, it is far more likely that they were a people—such as the Hurrites—in whom Indo-Aryan and Semitic elements had fused, to produce a degree of racial and cultural uniformity.

After the expulsion of the Hyksos (1546 B.C.) Egypt went through a period of great prosperity under Thutmose III and extended its boundaries to their maximum, to include Palestine and much of Syria. An impassible boundary to the north was the empire of the Hittites, with whom the successors of Thutmose had repeated clashes. Both these empires, however, were concerned for peace, and in 1270 B.C. they arrived at the famous agreement between Hattusil III and the Pharaoh Ramses II, which is described as one of the earliest treaties in history to come down to us in the original version.

While the Levant was preparing itself for peace, in the peninsulas and islands of the Mediterranean (Italy, Greece, Lycia, Cilicia, Crete, Cyprus) large-scale movements of peoples were taking place. It was a period, to use the cumbersome but expressive term of German historians, of *Völkerwanderung,* of "peoples moving, wandering,

26

changing place." Probably a series of mild summers in central Asia led to an increase in the flocks and herds on which the inhabitants depended, and groups of nomadic tribes began to push one another southward, toward the lands of the sun. These were inhabited by agricultural peoples, by builders of fortresses and cities, who tried to defend themselves but were mostly overwhelmed and dispersed.

The last wave of this movement of peoples lapped the eastern coasts of the Mediterranean. Around 1200 B.C. the "sea peoples," perhaps driven from Crete, from Hellas, and from Cyprus, appeared in Anatolia and Egypt. The Egyptian empire, after a series of struggles, was able largely to repulse the invaders, but the Hittite empire was overrun and within a few decades vanished from history, surviving only for a short time as a shadow of its former self in various minor kingdoms along the upper Euphrates.

Among the "peoples from the sea" the Egyptians name the Purusati (i.e., Philistines), possibly related to the Pelasgians, as well as the Sheklesh (which makes one think of Sicily) and the Shirdana, a possible reference to Sardinia. The Philistines first tried to occupy the fertile lands at the mouth of the Nile; driven back by the Egyptians, they moved off toward the coasts of the land of Canaan. Their cultural level and military organization were greatly superior to those of the peoples they encountered; so the Philistines managed to settle along the coast, to the south of Mount Carmel, without much difficulty, and gradually came to found a federation of five wealthy cities—Ashdod, Ascalon, Ekron, Gath, and Gaza—which was able to maintain some sort of independence until Roman times.

Who were the Philistines? Very probably a people speaking an Indo-European language, bringing with them elements of the culture that had flourished on the islands and coasts of the Mediterranean. In Egyptian bas-reliefs the Philistines were shown with a curious fringed headdress, reminiscent of those of the Lycians and the warriors of Mycenae. They brought iron weapons to Asia, and this immediately gave them an undisputed superiority among peoples who fought with bronze and who knew iron only as a costly rarity.

The Philistine invasion of the land they called Philistina (Palestine) had an important political consequence: it blocked Egypt's entry to Syria, or at least made it more difficult. Meanwhile in Anatolia the Hittite empire had fallen, while in Mesopotamia there was no hegemonic state, so that in the regions between the Dead Sea and the Mediterranean, between the Lebanon and Sinai, there was a considerable "power vacuum." The people who took advantage of this were those that certain Egyptian documents call Hapiru or Habiru, frequently identified with the Hebrews.

To ask who the Hebrews were and where they came from may seem too big a question; for those who follow the Bible literally it may also seem superfluous. Yet the Bible gives us many clues which imply the likelihood of a suggestion that the Hebrews originally came from Mesopotamia. The patriarch Terah, with his son Abram (later Abraham) and others of his family, started off from Ur of the Chaldees, the very first move in the century-long journey of the people toward the "Promised

City wall near Damascus Gate

Land," Canaan (Gen. 11:31). Among the descendants of Noah we find Nimrod, "a great hunter in the eyes of the Lord," the first to be "a mighty one in the earth" (Gen. 10:8). His empire extended to Babel (Babylonia), Erek, and Akkad, i.e., over a large part of Semitic Mesopotamia as historically opposed to Sumerian Mesopotamia. And it was in Babylonia (Babel) that the tower was built whose topmost pinnacle was to touch the heavens (Gen. 11:4). This was certainly a ziggurat of superimposed terraces. Today the steppes and sands of Iraq are scattered with the ruins of ziggurats; possibly the Bible was referring to the most famous of them all, which was called Etemenanki ("House of the foundation of Heaven and Earth") and was dedicated to the great god Marduk, protector of Babylon. The Bible gives details: "And they had brick for stone, and slime had they for mortar" (Gen. 11:3), hinting at an impressive technical detail of Babylonian building methods.

Typically Babylonian too was the predilection for the number seven, stemming from a Mesopotamian cosmological conception according to which the major stars (sun, moon, and five planets) acted continuously, favorably or unfavorably, on the fortunes of the world and its inhabitants. Finally, the idea of transferring the sins of the community onto an animal (usually a goat) was also Babylonian; the creature was then driven to die a wretched death in the desert, taking with it and expiating the evil committed by men (Lev. 16:20–22). This idea is still echoed in the Christian one of the Lamb of God, "which taketh away the sin of the world" (John 1:29), though the thought here is more complex and includes mystical strains deriving from the themes of the Servant of the Lord (Isa. 53:7) as well as from the paschal sacrifice (Exod. 12:1 ff.).

After they had left Mesopotamia it is probable that the Hebrews wandered at length in various groups throughout the valleys and mountains of Syria, the Lebanon, and the regions later to be called Palestine. The account of the wanderings of Abraham (nineteenth century B.C.?) may be a highly personalized echo of similar wanderings, just as those of Agamemnon and his friends, sung of by Homer, elaborate in a poetic form deeds actually though more anonymously carried out by the people known as the Achaeans, or Ahhiyava, depending on who it was who saw and encountered them.

By now it seems certain that, at least in small groups and at least in part, the Hebrews occupied the lands between Jordan and the sea from the middle of the second millennium B.C. If indeed the Habiru are the Hebrews, the tablets with cuneiform writing found at Tel el-Amarna tell us that they caused a lot of trouble for the rulers of the city-states of Canaan around 1360–50. In any case, the Bible, too, implies that many descendants of Abraham did not go to Egypt but stayed to pasture their herds in the lands of the East.

Much the most famous group of Hebrews is that which, at a certain moment (calculated to be about 1250 B.C.), left Egypt, where they had spent a long and harsh period of bondage, to head eastward, toward the Promised Land of Canaan. This wandering Hebrew people was headed by a charismatic leader of singular genius and

28

Right
Golden Gate, exterior wall

Next two pages
Golden Gate, interior wall

vigor—Moses—who tradition claims was in constant and direct contact with God. From heaven he received instructions on religious matters, cultural and moral decalogues, the elements of an entire legal system, the power to perform miracles. His name is revered by the Jews as that of the greatest man of all time. In the thirteen articles of faith, composed by Maimonides (1135–1204) in Arabic in his commentary on the Mishnah—articles which constitute, so to speak, the credo of Judaism—Moses is the only created being, apart from the anonymous future Messiah, regarded as worthy of being mentioned together with the Creator; he is the "greatest of the prophets."

The wanderings of the Jews in the desert, the exodus par excellence, lasted presumably more than forty years; the dramatic events of this experience, through which the children of Israel achieved supreme and final self-awareness, in which miracles, trials, victories, desperation, the wrath of God, cataclysms of nature, horrors and wonders follow one another in a story of the most vigorous liveliness, are part of the history of art, music, and folklore of the whole of the West. No one has gone through his childhood without encountering Moses causing water to spring from the rock, turning his rod into a serpent, receiving the tables of the law from a bearded Lord with a triangular halo, on the heights of Sinai, amid storm clouds, thunder, and a glory of light. Who could have grown up without ruminating over the Red Sea opening before the fleeing multitude, or over the manna spread throughout the desert like biscuits and dried figs? An inexhaustible source of images, inspired by similar subjects, has accompanied our culture through the centuries, from the early Christian catacombs and sarcophagi to Cecil B. De Mille and Hollywood epics, from Byzantine and Norman mosaics to Rouault and Chagall, from Raphael and Michelangelo to the comic strip, from Murillo to Poussin and Blake.

As has often been said, the most extraordinary feats, the most marvelous actions, are of little use to humanity unless someone perpetuates them in a book. There is no knowing how many heroes in the mists of time performed superhuman tasks, but only a few lucky ones like Achilles, Hector, Ulysses, Aeneas, Rustam, Turiel, Rama, and Lakshmana found Homers, Vergils, a Firdausi, Rustevel, or Valmiki to sing of them. There is no means of knowing how many peoples, in the dawn of distant ages, may have been through far more desperate and eventful exoduses than that of the Jews.

One need think only of the Huns, halted on the borders of China by the Han emperors and who reappeared at the gates of the Roman Empire ten generations later, or of certain Germanic peoples (like the Vandals) who within the space of a very few years migrated from the northern forests of Silesia to the parched deserts of Numidia.

None of them was able to count on the pen of a Yahwist or Elohist writer to recount episodes and anecdotes of their ups and downs to future generations.

The Bible, it is said, is still the world's bestseller, yet each generation assesses it in its own way. For centuries it was the source, not only of all knowledge about

29

Golden Gate, detail

the first and last things, but of all information about the earliest history of the Jewish people; then came historical criticism, the Tübingen school, the great dissecters of the Biblical text, such as Graf and Wellhausen, and within a short time the Book was transformed from a theological and cosmological enchiridion into a continent with a complex literary geology, where stratifications had been confused by catastrophes or bradyseisms, where even the fossils needed special inspection and sometimes correction. Poor Moses Maimonides. "It is obligatory to believe"—he had written in the twelfth century—"that the law, as we know it today, is that which was revealed to Moses. It is all Divine." What anguish he would have felt on contemplating the view that modern man has of the so-called "holy books."

Exodus is certainly the echo of an exodus that really took place, but one must bear in mind the intense propagandistic fervor of the pages in which it is celebrated so as not to be completely dazzled and overwhelmed. The same is true for the conquest of Canaan, told in the books of Joshua and Judges. Furthermore, the account in each of these books is somewhat different. In the first Joshua appears as a hero almost entirely responsible for the conquest, which he achieved in a single burst of energy, while in Judges there are echoes of a probably more likely process, of something far more gradual, in which there were successful and unsuccessful battles, in which certain areas were subjugated while others remained in the hands of the Canaanites. Great successes like those celebrated in the song of Deborah—perhaps the oldest part of the whole Bible—were not followed by developments favorable to the Hebrews, chiefly because each of the twelve tribes wanted to act independently and was jealous of the others. Only under the threat of mortal danger did the tribes humble themselves in agreeing to a common rule, as under the Judge, Gideon. This situation persisted throughout several generations, perhaps for a couple of centuries.

V | KINGS, IN GLORY AND IN DISTRESS

But the day came when it had to end. It was felt that the tribes must unite, elect a king, admit someone's superiority—or perish. And it was the Philistines of the coast who exerted the decisive pressure on the Hebrews of the mountains. In about 1050 the forces of Israel were routed by the Philistines at Aphek; the holy Ark fell into the hands of infidels, and the Jews had to admit ignominious defeat. Furthermore, the Ammonites of the northeast, seeing them in difficulties, attacked them treacherously, seizing further territory.

The monarchy emerged in this climate of national crisis. By now the Hebrews had such old and well-rooted traditions of pastoral and democratic, and therefore parochial, life, that most were horrified at the idea of monarchy. Also, Mosaic monotheism regarded its heavenly, invisible, and ever-present Lord as the true sovereign of the people; to set an earthly king up beside him almost smacked of impiousness. Arguments must have been prolonged and dogged on both sides. The pages of the Bible which deal with the election of Saul, of the tribe of Benjamin, to the position of king (First Book of Samuel) bear obvious marks of this; there is a great deal of information, but it is presented confusedly according to two versions which merge with one another: the pro- and the anti-monarchical. Finally the monarchical view prevailed, and before the tribes gathered at Gilgal (not far from Jericho) the prophet Samuel (also acknowledged as a judge in I Sam. 7:6, 15–17; 12:1–7) anointed Saul king of Israel. This was about 1030 B.C.

With Saul (who reigned circa 1030–1000) monarchy had its first trial. The new sovereign won important battles against the forces of Moab, Ammon, Edom, Bethrehob, the king of Zobah, the Amalekites, and the Philistines: "and whithersoever he turned himself, he vexed them" (I Sam. 14:47). He met with serious difficulties among his own people: persistent disagreement cut him off from Samuel, and there was a long period of rivalry with the young David, whose star was rising ineluctably. One has the impression that Saul was a greater sovereign than the pages of the Bible would have us believe. He was the victim of mainly negative judgment partly because, after so many victories, he committed suicide in the battle of Gilboa, won by the Philistines, partly because the final revisers of the Biblical texts concerning him either exalted Samuel to his detriment if they were anti-monarchist, or gave the limelight to the irresistible David if they were monarchists.

Lastly, one must remember that Saul belonged to one of the lesser tribes, that of Benjamin, while the Biblical texts were mostly compiled by men of the tribe of Judah.

31

According to the First Book of Samuel, the long crisis in which Saul was caught up during the last years of his reign was caused by the sudden decline in the favor he enjoyed in the eyes of the God of Israel. A very ancient and more or less constant doctrine, to be found in the less recent parts of the Bible, is that according to which every good in life represents a reward for good conduct, every ill a punishment for transgressions against the commands of the Lord. This was so for everyone, but in a particularly impressive and alarming way with regard to the charismatic leaders of the people. We encounter a similar idea at the source of the "heavenly mandate" theory on which the legitimacy of the Chinese emperors was based for thousands of years.

The events in Saul's case were typical. One fine day the Lord informed him, through the mouth of the prophet Samuel (a prophet is not so much someone who *foretells the future* as someone who "speaks for" God), that the time had come to punish the neighboring people of Amalek for having opposed the Israelites in the deserts of Sinai at a particularly difficult moment in the exodus from Egypt: "Now go and smite Amalek, and utterly destroy all that they have, and spare them not; but slay both man and woman, infant and suckling, ox and sheep, camel and ass" (I Sam. 15:3). Saul gathered together two hundred thousand men and annihilated the Amalekites, but he spared their king, Agag, and the more valuable livestock; so the God darkened, was offended, became furious. He took possession of Samuel and made him speak: "It repenteth me that I have set up Saul to be king." Exact divine orders had been to kill every living being, men and animals; but this had been done only in part, and therefore Saul was gravely at fault. It was true, as one learns soon afterward, that Saul had acted in good faith, intending to offer the enemies' cattle as a sacrifice to the Lord. But the Lord was firm and fierce: I do not want sacrifices, I want obedience; you are no longer king! In vain Saul asked Samuel to obtain his pardon from the Lord. Samuel, too, was hard as stone. All he conceded Saul was that his fall from grace would be kept secret for some time while plans were made for the succession. The episode ended with the alarming scene of a real human sacrifice, that of the trembling king of Amalek: "And Samuel hewed Agag in pieces before the Lord in Gilgal" (I Sam. 15:33).

After the fall of Saul—who, however, continued to reign in fact for a long time—the "heavenly mandate" was passed on to David.

David (in some ancient Semitic languages the name means commander, military leader) is a figure of such importance, both in the shifting and elusive—though totally real and vital—history of myths, and in the repertory of all the arts of the West, that it is necessary to give him a certain prominence.

Divine inspiration led Samuel to Bethlehem to look for the new king among the descendants of Jesse. Jesse had several sons, variously three, six, or eight according to the different versions. The gist of the story was this: all the elder brothers were examined and excluded, and then Samuel asked Jesse whether he had any more offspring in the house; then the youngest, David, was called in from the hills where

Dome of the Rock,
seen through the arches
in the northeast corner
of the elevation

he had been tending the sheep. David was a boy "ruddy, and withal of a beautiful countenance, and goodly to look to" (I Sam. 16:12). The God did not want any time wasted; "This is he," he said. Samuel anointed him, and "the Spirit of the Lord came upon David."

But the road to the throne was long. Oddly enough, the anointing seems to have remained a secret, a seed for future events; evidently Saul did not know anything about it. Almost by chance David—who was not only handsome and well built, but also a good musician—entered Saul's court as a harpist. Saul suffered from terrible crises of daunting melancholy; music consoled and cheered him. David obtained a position of great prestige: he became King Saul's much-loved armor-bearer. It is an odd situation—the king, as everyone believed him to be, was king only in appearance because he had lost "divine favor." He knew it, and was tormented by the fact, but evidently believed that he could share the secret with Samuel alone. Yet the young man, who was a mere armor-bearer in the eyes of the world, knew that he was predestined to be the future king.

There was no time for subtle contrasts of thought. The Philistines were pressing at the borders of Israel; David put down his harp and took up the sword. Then came the episode of the giant Goliath: a legend that probably sums up in one supreme categorical action numerous warlike deeds in which the young David distinguished himself. His valor and personal charm gained him the friendship of Jonathan, Saul's son. Saul, jealous of David's successes, promoted him *(ut amoveatur)* from armor-bearer to chiliarch, commander of a thousand soldiers. In this new position his successes continued. David was the man of the hour. Michal, Saul's daughter, fell desperately in love with him. The king, now jealous to the point of madness, felt that the time had come to rid himself of the young officer who had become so burdensome and dangerous. Yes, he said to him, you may have my daughter, but you must bring me one hundred Philistines' foreskins. David must have found the request absurdly easy, for shortly afterward he took Saul two hundred! Saul, alarmed, could do nothing but give Michal as wife to the new star of the tribe of Judah.

David could do no wrong. The people acclaimed him, women languished for him; as far as the Philistines were concerned, they had only to appear on the horizon for him to put them to flight, with greater success than all Saul's other servants. The king began to think that the spirit of the Lord had descended upon the young man. Jealousy was followed by fear, and an unbearable bitterness. Saul decided to make David "disappear." He brooded over the idea for some time, and one day while David was playing the harp, during one of his terrible fits of melancholy, he seized a javelin and tried to run it through his victim and pin him against a wall. David, accustomed to this and far worse from his combats with the Philistines, foiled Saul's attempt; the javelin ran into the wall. It was now quite clear that the two men could not continue to live together. This was the beginning of David's wanderings as an outlaw. By now his name held an irresistible fascination for the young people of Israel, and soon we find him with a following of four hundred—"every one that was

Dome of the Rock,
south view through the arches
on top of the southwest steps

in distress, and every one that was in debt, and every one that was discontented" (I Sam. 22:2). Saul was furious. Unable to seize David, he put to death anyone found helping him in his flight. Adventures followed one another in rapid succession. David and his supporters conquered bands of Philistines and seized the small town of Keilah, which they subsequently had to abandon. One moment fate favored the king, the next it favored the rebel. David was alone again, driven from mountain to mountain. Then fortune suddenly offered him the means of killing Saul: the two men found themselves face to face in a cave. David could simply have brought down his sword upon his adversary's neck. But there were too many bonds between them. Saul was the father of Michal, his wife, and of his friend Jonathan; above all, he was the king, or at least everyone so regarded him, and to kill him would have been to shatter the established order, to offend the Lord. David put his sword back in its scabbard.

After further complicated adventures, other marriages, other raids and counter-raids in Bedouin territories, David sought refuge with the king of the enemy race of Philistines. There followed a period of somewhat obscure coexistence: the Philistines did not have much trust in David, and David plainly did not have the heart to fight against his own people alongside their hereditary enemies. It was in these difficult circumstances that the battle of Gilboa took place; the Philistines were victorious, and Jonathan and Saul died. David was deeply shaken and, at the moment of his most intense grief, wrote a memorable song, among the most beautiful in the Bible.

David, now about thirty years old, felt that the moment had come to take a step forward: he settled at Hebron, in the mountains of Judaea, and once again received holy unction from the "men of Judah" (II Sam. 2:4). Saul's inheritance had gone to his son Ish-bosheth, a weak and colorless man. But Ish-bosheth did have a strong military commander named Abner, and he therefore represented a considerable obstacle. There followed seven years, and more, during which there were bloody clashes between the two parties, while complex plots developed between Abner, as commander of Ish-bosheth's forces, and Joab, the commander of David's. Abner killed Joab's brother, Joab took revenge by killing Abner; David wanted to punish Joab but he was too valuable, and he had to forgive him. Ish-bosheth, deprived of Abner's help, fell victim to a plot. The way was clear. Even the northern tribes swore fidelity to David. The whole people of Israel, for the first time, had a universally acclaimed leader.

That the conquest of Canaan should have come about, not as the Book of Joshua said, all at once, but gradually, reducing the territories over which the sovereignty of the twelve tribes could be regarded as undisputed within the space of about two centuries, from 1250 to 1000 B.C., is shown by the fact that, even at this later date, when David was reigning from "Dan to Beersheba" and from the borders of the Dead Sea to the borders of Philistia, there still existed in the center of his kingdom an undefeated, independent city-fortress: Jebus (Jerusalem). David saw that, by con-

34

quering it, he could not only further increase his prestige but also gain the advantage of possessing a capital that was easy to fortify and embellish. The Jebusites, masters of the stronghold, were so convinced of the impregnability of their position that they would say: "The blind and lame alone can defend it!" And indeed so they might have done if David had not known of the existence of a hidden canal, providing communication between the citadel and the spring of Gihon. He sent a small group of men (led by Joab) along this narrow passage to take the defenders by surprise. The plan worked. David was master of Jebus—Jerusalem.

Unlike Saul, who had been recognized as king against the will of several of the twelve tribes, David had the unconditional support of both the tribes of the north, the most important of which was Ephraim, and those of the south, where Judah was dominant. Jerusalem was ideally situated, being near the border between the lands of Judah and those of Benjamin (King Saul's tribe). Furthermore, having been conquered by David himself, the new city was outside tribal territories; it became immediately a sort of District of Columbia, seat of the central government in a confederation of tribes.

David had shown great patience in his rise to power; once he had reached his goal, he determined to turn the fortress of the Jebusites into a brilliant city with all speed. After strengthening the defenses on Mount Ophel, he built himself a palace, mainly from cedars of Lebanon, which exerted an extraordinary fascination on the rulers of antiquity. Even in the epic of Gilgamesh, when the hero and his inseparable friend Enkidu dream of "performing immortal tasks," what do they settle upon? Going up to Lebanon to bring down cedar trunks! One of the reasons the pharaohs were so eager to extend their own sovereignty beyond Palestine, into Syria, was to ensure access to the forests of Lebanon. To be able to boast of cedar beams from Lebanon in one's palace was, in those times, to claim the supreme symbol of success in worldly affairs. David plainly had few workers sufficiently skilled to work wood and metal, however, because the Book of Samuel says that he had some sent from Hiram, king of Tyre, in Phoenicia.

Jerusalem was to become not only the king's impressive capital but also the religious and spiritual center of the Jewish people. David had the Ark of the Lord solemnly transported there, removing it from the small town of Baale where it was, and placing it in a special pavilion on a hill in the capital.

The ruler's life now became a shifting pattern of wars and passions. The Ammonites and Edomites were confronted and conquered, thanks mainly to Joab, the brave and skilled commander of David's forces. Meanwhile, in Jerusalem the king, strolling on a terrace of his new palace, saw in the distance a very beautiful woman, bathing; he made inquiries and learned that she was Bathsheba, the wife of a Hittite named Uriah. David conceived a violent passion for the woman. He met her secretly, and Bathsheba became pregnant. Uriah was sent to war against the Ammonites, and he died in a skirmish. When Uriah was dead, buried, and duly lamented by his widow, Bathsheba became David's queen, and gave birth to a son. "But the thing that David

35

Dome of the Rock, south view
Dome of the Chain, seen through the arches

had done displeased the Lord" (II Sam. 11:27), and the prophet Nathan brought him a divine message, taking the king severely to task for taking "the poor man's lamb" (II Sam. 12). David confesses his sin, and the Lord does not take his life, not even his kingship, but the author of the Book of Samuel ascribes all the tribulations which later were to befall David's family life to this event, and particularly the early death of the beloved child, the fruit of this sinful passion. Only afterward did Bathsheba give birth to David's favorite son and successor, Solomon.

By now David—conqueror of neighboring peoples on all sides—was ruler of a state that extended well beyond Damascus, to Sinai and the Red Sea, including the lands of Transjordan. He could justly consider that he had completely fulfilled the hopes of his people regarding the "Promised Land."

But the king's life had its darker side too. David, rather like Saul, did not meet his greatest troubles in politics, but in his home and with his own family. His sons, children of different mothers, were restless and violent; incestuous love and desire for vendetta united and divided them. Lastly Absalom, the third and one of the best-loved, revolted against his father, leading a breakaway movement. Conquered in battle, he was killed by Joab, to his father's great grief.

Other events saddened David's old age: the hatred of the descendants of Saul, against whom he took fierce, indeed excessive, measures; quarrels about the succession, which was given to Solomon, Bathsheba's son, bypassing the older Adonijah. During these years David, the shining young warrior, the enchanter of women, the singer who, like Orpheus, brought peace to troubled minds, the chivalrous commander who spared his enemy Saul when his life was within his grasp, had gradually become a suspicious, vindictive old man. Shortly before he died he advised his successor to put Joab to death—Joab, the general to whom he owed so large a part of his own success.

These late-evening shadows detract little from the greatness of the figure of David, who lived in times when life was envisaged according to principles of primeval harshness, very different from those of later and more mature centuries. Rather than the history of David, it is the myth of David that echoes down the centuries. In Chronicles he already appears as a warrior-saint; and an enormous number of psalms, many of which he certainly did not write, are attributed to him. In times of national strife, of humiliation and misery, his memory was projected into the future; David became the prototype of the Messiah, above all of the armed Messiah, the military leader descending in glory from the clouds to tame the enemies of Israel and establish a new order in the world.

This is the David whom the Christian West has inherited from Israel. His image is present throughout the Middle Ages. A hidden similarity between David and Siegfried made him particularly dear to the people of the North. In the Renaissance the myth of David merged with that of Apollo, and Michelangelo unconsciously gave supreme formal expression to this confluence.

David had made of Jerusalem the capital of a kingdom such as Palestine had

36

Dome of the Rock,
porch at main entrance

never seen before or since; he had given a worthy seat to the kings who were to govern it, he had tried to fuse the various tribes of Israel, to unite the Jebusites of the conquered city with the Israelites who had come there from outside; he had also brought the Ark to Jerusalem, making Mount Zion sacred to the Lord. Only one important plan had still to be carried out: the building of a temple dedicated to the Lord which would be worthy of the One God, of him who had brought the Hebrews safely out of distant Egypt and given them the Promised Land.

According to a tradition recounted in the Bible (I Chron. 21:18), David went up to one of the hills of Jerusalem where Ornan the Jebusite had a threshing floor. Even today, visiting the Dome of the Rock, on the great wind-swept terrace full of light and sky, one need only half close one's eyes to imagine this place as it must have been in that distant past. Beneath the marble which has felt the tread of janissaries and dervishes, Crusader kings and foreign counts, caliphs, imams, and sheiks, patriarchs and Eastern empresses, Roman consuls and flamens, Pharisees and Zealots, Sadducees and Essenes, philosophers and diadochi, Magi and satraps, High Priests and kings of Judah, beneath it all, before it all, there was a spacious threshing floor with ears of wheat spread in the sun, beasts to tread them, women with children in their arms. "Ornan looked and saw David... and bowed himself to David with his face to the ground. Then David said to Ornan, Grant me the place of this threshing floor, that I may build an altar therein unto the Lord: thou shalt grant it me for the full price: that the plague may be stayed from the people. And Ornan said unto David, Take it to thee, and let my lord the king do that which is good in his eyes: lo, I give thee the oxen also for burnt offerings, and the threshing instruments for wood, and the wheat for the meat offering; I give it all. And King David said to Ornan, Nay; but I will verily buy it for the full price: for I will not take that which is thine for the Lord, nor offer burnt offering without cost. So David gave to Ornan for the place six hundred shekels of gold by weight." An altar was erected on Ornan's old threshing floor and sacrifices were offered to the Lord. Then David collected an impressive quantity of materials for this work that was to be so magnificent: iron, bronze, cedar trunks in abundance, stones of all kinds. The Temple, said David, must be "magnifical, of fame and glory throughout all countries." But the days of the sovereign were numbered. The completion of the Temple became the task of his successor Solomon, the "Peaceful," as his name means in Hebrew.

The reign of Solomon (970–936) began, if not with a bloodbath, at least with a series of acts of violence. The succession had been much disputed. Adonijah, Solomon's elder half-brother, had been excluded from the throne. His resentment— and that of his supporters—was not to be allayed: "All Israel set their faces on me, that I should reign" (I Kings 2:15). When Adonijah asked Solomon to give him Abishag, their father's last and very beautiful concubine, matters came to a head, and Adonijah paid with his life. According to the Jewish custom of the time, whoever managed to gain a hold over the king's women, and to cohabit with them, had a strong right to succession to the throne. Absalom had already tried to make use of

37

Marble pulpit,
Haram-ash-Sharif

this right at the time of his revolt against his father, David. A tent had been put up on the terrace of the royal dwelling, "and Absalom went in unto his father's concubines in the sight of all Israel" (II Sam. 16:22). But all the scheme accomplished for Absalom was to assuage his desire and pride for a few hours. Things went even less well for Adonijah: he had not even managed to lay a finger on Abishag before Solomon had him murdered by the new star of the moment, Benaiah, who shortly afterward became head of the royal army.

Joab too, the old general who had won so many battles for King David, was put to death. True, his life was now in jeopardy anyway, because of the killings of Abner and Amasa, but his tragic end, dramatically described in the Book of the Kings, is nonetheless deeply moving. One immediately thinks of Parmenio, who had been the companion first of Philip of Macedon, then of Alexander the Great, in all their victories, and whom Alexander himself had put to death. But the circumstances were altogether different. Parmenio died because of a sudden suspicion on the part of the Greek king; Joab's fate was linked to a whole subtle and inexorable mechanism of blood-feud customs. Vendetta was fully accepted by the ethics of the time, but it had to respect certain forms; Joab had not respected them, and thus stained the military honor of the king. The vendetta had therefore developed into a new debt of blood, which weighed upon the king and on his descendants. There was no way out but to sacrifice the original culprit, Joab. In vain he sought refuge at the altar in the tent of the Lord so that Solomon's name would be stained with the shame of profaning a holy place; he was struck down all the same.

But this beginning, which might have presaged a reign full of all kinds of violence, was followed by prosperous and luxurious decades of peace. If David had been the sovereign of the sword, Solomon was the sovereign of treaties, alliances, peaceful compromises. David's first concern was territorial expansion; Solomon's main interest was the economy. David's years were marked by the poetry of bloodshed, valor, music; those of Solomon, by the prose of wisdom and of gold.

The Judgment of Solomon, King Solomon's mines, the riches of Solomon, Solomon marrying the daughter of the Pharaoh of Egypt, Solomon and the Queen of Sheba—these are some of the three-thousand-year-old echoes that are part of the best-loved Western traditions; events that have become proverbs, themes that have inspired painters, musicians, novelists, film-makers. In his own life Solomon gave proof of the whole range of those gifts which, thousands of years later, were to burgeon in the Rothschilds, the Duveens, the Kresses. He allied himself with the Phoenicians, the Egyptians, sent his ships as far as Tarshish, in Spain, at that time regarded as the end of the earth, bought horses from the nomads of the north and exported them to the kingdoms of the south, importing rare woods and precious metals in exchange. When the Bible (First Book of the Kings) tells of Solomon, it sounds like a fairy tale—or a newspaper account of the crowning of the Shah of Persia: the hundreds of gold shields decorating the palace, the great House of the Forest of Lebanon with its cedar pillars ("Nothing like it had been seen in any kingdom"), the stables (fourteen hun-

38

Capital of marble pulpit,
Haram-ash-Sharif

dred carriages, twelve hundred horses), the fleet. Silver, however, was not even considered in those days of plenty.

The splendor of the palace was equaled by the richness of the harem. Solomon welcomed beautiful women from all countries with the eagerness of a collector seeking rare objects to delight him: there were Ammonites, Edomites, Phoenicians, Hittites, Philistines, Cretans, Aryans, Hurrites from the Caucasus, Nubians. And here the Biblical chronicler, always ready to find the remote roots of decline, defeat, and national disaster in an offense to God, notes that, of the king's seven hundred wives and three hundred concubines, there were many who managed to "turn away his heart after other gods" (I Kings 11:4). If Gobineau and Chamberlain explain history in racial terms, if the Marxists see the roots of all development and upheaval in economics and technology, the authors of the Biblical texts interpreted the destiny of their people in the light of a single oscillating factor: that of the favor or wrath of their God. The people behave well, worship the true God, blessings abound; they become lazy, forget and betray him, they are cursed and punished. The cycle has the detached awesomeness of a law of nature.

Solomon, like Herod, was a tireless builder: he extended, embellished, and partly rebuilt the royal palace, and during his reign the fortifications of Jerusalem were made more extensive and formidable than before. His main work was the building of the Temple, which took up a good seven years of his reign (959–952 B.C.). A temple, for the Jews, was not simply the "house of God" but a vast enclosed area with a variety of buildings, as is still the case today in southern India, Cambodia, and the Buddhist countries of the Far East. Mount Moriah, with the threshing floor bought by David, must have been rather irregular. A flat space was obtained partly, perhaps, by leveling the top of the hill, partly by reinforcing its sides with masonry. Beyond these walls were huge empty spaces, crypts, today known as "Solomon's stables"; but the name is misleading, and their present shape dates back to a far less remote time, possibly that of Herod.

The Temple itself was built inside the sacred enclave, facing east. There can have been no shortage of labor in Jerusalem, and we know that it was the Jews themselves who built it, but technicians and artists came from outside, from the cities of Phoenicia. What did the Temple of Solomon look like? It can be reconstructed ideally from a wealth of data, some of them very precise, to be found in the Biblical texts. It probably was not very big (about 40 by 13 yards) and was apparently divided—like the Egyptian temples from which it was basically derived—into three sections: a porch (*ulam*) to which the ordinary mass of the faithful were admitted; a hall, the "holy place" (*hekal*), to be entered only by the priests; and a Holy of Holies (*debir*), small, square, and windowless, which housed the tables of the Law—graven by God himself and delivered to Moses—and which could be entered by the High Priest only, once a year, on the Day of Atonement.

The Temple of Solomon remained standing almost four hundred years, until 587 B.C., the fateful date when Nebuchadnezzar, heading the Babylonian forces, took

39

Fountain of Qait Bey
and Gate of Cotton Bazaar

Jerusalem and destroyed the building. Its foundations lay near the rock of Abraham's sacrifice, or possibly actually around this stone. In its building the architects had used beams of cedar and cypress, fine stone, and the ornaments were of bronze and rare metals. Within the Temple precincts were precious religious objects, including the "sea of brass," a circular vessel with a diameter of about four yards, supported by twelve bronze oxen, which held the water for ablutions. On a great altar, also of bronze, animal sacrifices were offered; there were also minor altars for bread offerings, and for incense.

Despite the brilliance of his court and his new capital of Jerusalem, Solomon's reign, particularly during the last years, showed signs of serious weakness. The neighboring kingdoms—especially those of Edom and of the Aramaeans (Damascus)—were growing stronger, the cost of the embellishments and fortifications of the capital fell increasingly heavily upon the people, and the old tribalism once again became a centrifugal factor, particularly because Solomon and those close to him, perhaps without foreseeing the consequences of such behavior, favored the members of the tribe of Judah to the detriment of those of the sister tribes.

On his death, Solomon left the succession to his son Rehoboam. There was a grand council of the tribes at Shechem, where, if Rehoboam had known how to proceed with tact, he might have retained the whole of his father's inheritance. For a long time the northern tribes, with Ephraim at their head, had clearly been unhappy about the real or imaginary abuses of power perpetrated by the tribe of Judah. Rehoboam was asked to review all his father's agreements and to lighten taxes and obligations. The colorful account in the Book of the Kings credits Rehoboam with a cutting reply: "My father made your yoke heavy, but I will chastise you with scorpions" (I Kings 12:14). Indignantly the tribes of the north shouted: "To your tents, O Israel; now see to thine own house, David."

This was schism, the division of the state into two (931 B.C.). To the north was a larger, more populous, stronger kingdom, which kept the name of Israel; to the south, a smaller state consisting of the tribes of Judah, Benjamin, and in part the Levites, but a very compact state, and one that included the stronghold of Jerusalem, the holy city. The division of David's heritage was the seed of the troubles that were to hound the Hebrew world in the centuries to come. As we have seen, Palestine lay caught between the naturally bounded territories of great and strong empires: Egypt on the one hand and Mesopotamia on the other. David's kingdom had arisen, and had been able to last for a certain time, because of the power vacuum that had occurred in Syria, when Egypt and Mesopotamia both underwent a period of crisis. This favorable situation could not last long. Under Shishak (reigned 935–919), founder of the 22nd dynasty, Egypt very soon regained its former vigor; only a little later the Assyrians, under Adad-nirari II (912–891), began a movement of expansion which continued under Tiglath-pilezer III and his successors, until the time of Ashurbani-

40

pal—perhaps the Sardanapalus of Greek historians. If the Jewish people had been united in a single political organism, perhaps they would have been able to resist, but divided into two kingdoms, and in addition often fighting among themselves, they were bound to be overrun and destroyed.

Just a few years after the council of Shechem, the Pharaoh Shishak occupied Jerusalem for a short time (927 B.C.), sacking the Temple of the treasures that Solomon had collected there. In 790 B.C. Jerusalem was attacked again, this time by the forces of Israel, led by King Joash. Meanwhile, the Assyrians were at the gates of Palestine, and in 722 B.C. Shalmaneser V was beneath the walls of Samaria, the capital of the kingdom of Israel. The Assyrian king died during the siege; he was succeeded by Sargon II, who forced the city to surrender and destroyed it. This was the end of the kingdom of Israel. Furthermore, the Assyrians, in their usual cruel fashion, deported almost all the Jews, scattering them throughout their Mesopotamian lands, and replaced them with people of other races. Ten tribes of the Hebrew people were declared "lost" henceforth; the Samaritans were from now on a bastard branch of the Hebrews, having effected a religious secession regarded with suspicion and often with disdain by the others.

It is interesting to note that the Samaritans still exist. There are very few of them, about four hundred, concentrated mainly in the city of Nablus (near the Biblical Shechem), at the foot of Mount Gerizim, which they believed to be the holy place chosen by the Lord (i.e., in disagreement with the Jews, who believe that their God had chosen Mount Zion: "The Lord is great in Zion" [Ps. 99:2]). The smaller part of the Samaritan community lives in the Israeli town of Holon, near Tel Aviv, and even during the partition of the Holy Land they were permitted to join their brethren in Nablus, then Jordanian, once a year for the Passover Sacrifice, celebrated on Mount Gerizim according to the archaic Biblical rites. The Samaritan Biblical canon is very simple, consisting only of the Pentateuch and the Book of Joshua, which they have preserved in a version slightly different from the Jewish one and from the ancient Greek translation, known as the Septuagint. The only prophet they recognize is Moses, with whom their expected Messiah—or rather restorer of the period of Divine Pleasure—is usually identified.

The Samaritans have a curious vision of history, which they divide into a period of Divine Pleasure (Aramaic: *Rahuta*), starting with the creation of the world and characterized by the presence in Israel of the true tabernacle, containing the Ark with the sacred vessels, and a period of Divine Displeasure or, to use an expression of Martin Buber, of God's Eclipse (Aramaic: *Fanuta*), which began at the moment of the mysterious disappearance of those vessels, 260 years after the entry of the children of Israel into the Holy Land (972 B.C.). This is reminiscent of the three periods which the thirteenth-century Japanese Buddhist reformer Nichiren sees in the history of man: *Shōbō*, the period of the Real Law, *Zōbō*, the period of the Reflected Law, and *Mappō*, the age of the Destruction of the Law. The idea, essential to Judaism and Christianity, too, is that man is a fallen creature, a being undergoing punishment, who

41

Fountain,
Haram-ash-Sharif

has fallen from a state of beatitude and rectitude into one of misery and evil-doing: just the opposite of one of the favorite ideas of modern man—that our species is emerging from a distant past of ignorance and impotence and is marching toward a future of wisdom and well-being.

The small kingdom of Judaea, left on its own, managed to survive, through various vicissitudes, for another hundred and thirty-five years. This was a period of a marked political and military recovery, both in Egypt and in Assyria. The Jewish kings fortified Jerusalem several times. One of them, Hezekiah (716–687), had the daring idea of building an aqueduct, the greater part of which ran through a tunnel dug out of the rock, carrying the waters of Gihon to Siloam, thus ensuring a reliable water supply for the inhabitants in case of siege.

It is probable that Hezekiah's conduit, and the impressive fortifications of Jerusalem (not to mention a timely and unhoped-for outbreak of plague among the besiegers), saved the holy city from the attack in 701 B.C. of a new Assyrian king, Sennacherib. After this Assyrian failure Jerusalem must have become known as an impregnable fortress. For over a century the city was able to flourish, almost undisturbed, as a trading center and goal of religious pilgrimages. Meanwhile, in Mesopotamia events of the greatest importance were taking place. The age-old rivalry between Babylonia and Assyria, which led to the alternating supremacy of one or the other, underwent a sudden reversal as the Assyrians, who had come to seem the unconquerable masters, were overthrown by Nebupolassar, the founder of a new Babylonian empire. This vast and famous empire lasted only eighty-six years (625–539), but it was during this short period, particularly under Nebuchadnezzar, that Babylon achieved the greatness, the wealth and splendor, that made it one of the great cities of history.

The kings of Judaea tried to resist the neo-Babylonian advance by calling on the Egyptians for help; but they had not fully reckoned with the power of their enemies from the east. Jerusalem was besieged and taken on two occasions, first in 597 B.C., when the king, court, and all the ruling class were deported, and again in 587— after a subsequent revolt—when it was burned and destroyed.

42

VI | DEEP DOWN, UNDER MOUNT OPHEL

In summer Jerusalem is cool, amazingly cool considering its latitude. Its position on a hilltop at an altitude of twenty-five hundred feet means that it always gets a breeze either from the sea or from the north; in the evening when the sun sets you are glad of a jacket or sweater. At night, in bed, you need a blanket.

But there are brutal, sultry days—particularly when the *khamsin* blows in from the desert. One day in particular I remember. A veiled sun, a monstrous bubble of yellow light, beat down insistently on the stones of the city and on that fine, almost white dust that the slightest breath of wind sends whirling up into the air.

Someone said: Let's go to Hezekiah's conduit!

This was how we came to be at the pool of the Virgin, known in Arabic as the Um-ed-Daraj, in Biblical writings as Gihon. We were in the valley of Kedron; above us the walls of Jerusalem towered like a great fortress. We had taken bathing suits, rubber-soled canvas shoes, and, of course, flashlights. We also had a couple of cameras.

The Gihon pool, or spring, is a very important point in the topography of Jerusalem. Here the inhabitants had a permanent and abundant supply of excellent fresh water. From the earliest times the spring had communicated with the upper part of the city by means of an underground passage—which, according to the traditional interpretation, was used by Joab and his men for the taking of the Jebusite fortress.

In the last years of the eighth century B.C., when the Assyrian king, Sennacherib, was advancing threateningly toward Jerusalem, Hezekiah, king of Judah (reigned 725–697 B.C.), planned what was a most extraordinary undertaking for those times: the digging of a tunnel, six hundred yards long, out of the rock of Mount Ophel, to bring the water from the Gihon spring to that of Siloam (II Chron. 32:30). The spring of Gihon was apparently difficult to defend, while Siloam was in a much safer spot, particularly in the event of a long siege. Possibly a series of fractures in the rock guided and facilitated the work of the excavators, and the limestone of the hill was not excessively hard. The fact remains that within a relatively short time the work was completed and a six-hundred-yard tunnel joined the two springs.

Just as is done today, the work was begun from the two ends and excavation moved forward to a likely meeting place for the two teams of miners deep in the earth. In about 1880 a stone was discovered in the tunnel, bearing an inscription in ancient Hebrew recording for posterity the moving moment when the two groups of men came face to face. Now that we have sophisticated instruments of all kinds at

43

Little dome near north wall,
Haram-ash-Sharif

our disposal, when the most expert qualified engineers direct the workmen, such a thing is only to be expected, but in those remote days over sixteen centuries ago it must have been an inspiring moment, almost miraculous. The inscription itself is sober, a simple statement of fact, but it speaks more vividly than any piece of rhetoric. This is what it says: "... and this is the story of the piercing. While [the hewers were lifting] their axes one man against his companion and while three cubits remained to pierce, [there was heard] the voice of one man calling to his companion, for there was a crevice in the rock to the right and the left. And on the day of piercing the hewers struck one man against his companion, ax against ax, and the waters went from the spring to the pool two hundred and a thousand cubits. And one hundred cubits was the height of the rock above the head of the hewers...."

When we arrived at the pool of the Virgin we went down a steep flight of steps toward a dark cave; here we undressed and prepared to enter the water flowing just below us, beyond an open iron gate. As we were finishing our preparations, stuffing our clothes into rucksacks we could carry on our backs during the journey, two other people appeared, a young English girl and an Israeli. We decided to carry on together; there were five of us, some with flashlights, some with candles—it was like a visit to the catacombs.

Now we were face to face with the water. It welled in the dark from the rock, cold and plentiful, gleaming and clear in the rays of the flashlights. I must admit frankly that I sighed with relief. For some reason I had imagined Hezekiah's conduit as muddy, with sluggish, greenish water, the invisible bottom strewn with refuse.

We were now right in the underground canal. The water soon came up to our knees, then almost to our waists. It was marvelously cool! You needed an exceptionally hot day for this visit, and I think that at other times of the year you would need fisherman's hip boots.

We walked in Indian file, holding our flashlights. The tunnel is made with great care and precision. The depth of the water, after a few initial irregularities, had become constant at knee height. Around us, in the rock, we could see traces of the old picks; in some places the strokes had been so regular that they had produced a geometrical motif, a chiseling repeated with extreme patience. Often the tunnel curved, now to the left and now to the right. Had the excavators indeed followed a natural series of fissures? Otherwise, would they not have proceeded in a straight line?

In the first half the roof of the tunnel is low almost all the time; at some points you have to lower your head a little to go forward. I had read that it was hard to get through, that you had to go "along certain parts on your knees or stomach." Bearing in mind certain experiences in speleology, I had imagined all manner of tight spots, but nothing of the kind; the tunnel is surprisingly easy and regular, so that you find yourself constantly thinking with admiration of the men who conceived of and realized such a feat of engineering.

Every so often I noticed natural fissures opening upward in the rock. There are also traces of work broken off, of corrections, second thoughts in the plan of the

44

tunnel. After some time we arrived at the place where the two teams had met. The voices of Rosemary and her friend resounded ahead of us with strange, deep echoes; there was no other sound except the almost imperceptible murmur of the water flowing in its bed, darker than the rest of the rock because of the presence of micro-organisms. We began to feel thoroughly chilled.

More than halfway along the tunnel I noted a curious feature: the passage, though still the same in width, had a higher ceiling; at some points it positively vanished above one's head into a darkness dispelled only by the direct rays of a flashlight. It is as though the team which had been advancing from below, from the spring of Siloam, had calculated the direction exactly, but not the inclination, of its own stretch. Probably when the two groups met the upper one came out below, so that it had been necessary to deepen the passage dug from below, and quite considerably in certain parts.

By now a good half hour had passed since we entered the tunnel. Suddenly we felt welcome bursts of warm dry air.... Now we were all thinking of a good "scorching khamsin afternoon"!

Several steps more and we heard voices, then saw light. Finally we went through a second iron gate, also open, and came out up the steps of Siloam. How beautiful light is! We felt we were experiencing the joy of the blind man to whom, according to tradition, Jesus gave back his sight on this very spot (John 9:7–41).

45

VII | "I HAVE FOUND THE BOOK OF THE LAW"

These centuries were rich in spiritual movements, decisive in the development of the Jewish faith and the Jewish spirit. One must not be misled by the Biblical texts which tell the stories of the origins of the Jewish people (Pentateuch, Joshua, Judges); for the most part these express ideas projected back in time from those already mature centuries into an archaic dawn. From the monarchy onward, from the moment when, presumably, facts were registered more or less accurately, the texts themselves show us how difficult, complex, and laborious was the establishing of monotheistic worship in men's souls and in ritual. Much blame was laid upon women (the foreign wives of Solomon; Jezebel, the Phoenician princess, who married King Ahab of Israel; Athaliah, queen of Judah, and so on) who—it was said—introduced "abominable" cults from outside: those of Astarte, Tammuz, Baal. Some of those cults were truly abominable (for instance, the cult of Moloch, which required the burning, possibly alive, of first-born children in sacrifice to the god). But these women would never have had such power over men if the cult of the one God had really been deeply and firmly rooted.

During these agitated centuries (eleventh to sixth B.C.) the movement of the prophets, of those who "speak for God," emerged and flourished. There had already been prophets (and prophetesses—Deborah) contemporary with the Judges, but Samuel, who anointed Saul and David, was the first of a series of giants. He was followed by Elijah, the rough mountain dweller of Gilead, who walked the stage of contemporary history amid prophecies and epiphanies, prodigies and miracles, resurrecting the dead, causing flour and oil to multiply, slaying false prophets and the king's guards sent out to arrest him, purifying wells, feeding inconvenient little boys to bears, and finally disappearing upward in a celestial whirlwind in a chariot drawn by fiery horses. Elijah left his mantle and succession to Elisha. After Elisha came the prophets who dictated or wrote, Amos, Hosea, and the great ones: Isaiah and Jeremiah, who take us up to the fall of Jerusalem. Lastly, Ezekiel and Daniel, who were active during and after the period of exile.

In the political, social, and economic fields, the Biblical texts pose rather than solve problems, but in the field of religion they offer a vast and immensely detailed picture of their times. The main actors in the great drama, partly played out on the cosmic level, are on the one hand the Lord, with his commands, proclamations, revelations, promises, loves, hates, curses, celebrations, and rewards, and on the other the rulers, the peoples of Judah and Israel, who sometimes follow the paths of holiness but sometimes forsake them to sin, to bow their heads to other gods, to

46

honor those who should be execrated, to offer abominable sacrifices and perform foul rites. Indeed, the relations between Israel and her God have the fire, the languors, pangs, and anguish of a passionate love affair. It has been determined that the main body of the Song of Songs is composed of old wedding chants which were sung during the "king's week" when, amid festivities and dancing by friends and relatives, the groom acted the part of the king, the bride that of the queen. But the classical, Judaic interpretation—that the groom represents God and the bride Israel—corresponds perfectly, if not to the intentions of the writer of the poem, at least to the psychological reality of the marriage between God and people. Between the Lord and the people stood the figure of the prophet, the living incarnation of the collective Conscience.

The triangle composed of the Lord God, the sovereign-sinner, and the prophet who warns, condemns, threatens, rebukes, and pardons, was established from the times of the first great kings. A typical episode was the census of David. According to the ideas of the time, to take a census of the people was an act of impiety; it was considered to infringe upon the prerogatives of God, who alone was responsible for the increase of men and their families. At one point King David was evilly inspired, either by the "anger of the Lord" (II Sam. 24:1) or by Satan (I Chron. 21:1), and took a census of the people (which apparently numbered one million, three hundred thousand men fit to bear arms, a figure far greater than anything probable at the time). Having completed what today would be considered as an act of wise administrative policy, David was seized by fear: "I have sinned greatly...." Indeed, a prophet soon informed him that God had been offended, and that the people should be prepared for vengeance. David could choose: either three years of famine, or three months of military defeat, or three days of plague. David chose plague (in which seventy thousand men died, according to the Second Book of Samuel). Furthermore, the Lord "stretched out his hand upon Jerusalem, to destroy it," though luckily he took pity at the last moment. "That is enough!" he shouted from heaven to the angel of death, who was wandering about bringing death through the mountains of Israel: "Stay now thy hand, for the moment." It was on this occasion that David took the first step toward founding the Temple of his new capital.

Almost every chapter in the Books of the Kings and Chronicles, which closely follow the history of the kingdoms of Israel and Judah, recounts incidents that fit into the God-prophet-king triangle. Israel seemed to live under the threat of an original sin which brought the worst possible troubles upon her: that of having separated from the main and legitimate line of descendance from Solomon. This division had also entailed a splitting up of the holy places and a lessening of the primacy of Jerusalem. Furthermore, in the holy places of the north, Bethel and Dan, God was worshiped in the form of golden calves. Quite probably this was a survival of ancient pagan cults: the priests said that the calf was just the visible mount of an invisible god, something like the *vahana* (vehicle) of the Heavenly Buddhas in the Mahayanic iconography. The most scrupulous religious tradition regarded this

47

Doorway painted for reception of
Moslem pilgrims returning from Mecca

worship as a very serious sin, great enough to justify the worst disasters and final destruction of the kingdom: "Woe to the crown of pride, to the drunkards of Ephraim, whose glorious beauty is a fading flower," Isaiah thundered (Isa. 28:1), and Amos foretold blood, tears, and extinction.

An equally lamentable fate awaited Judah, if it did not mend its ways, which it showed no signs of doing. King Manasseh in particular (687–642 B.C.) did "that which was evil in the sight of the Lord," imitating the abominations of the peoples "whom the Lord had cast out before the children of Israel" (II Chron. 33:2). At the foot of the hill of Jerusalem, to the southwest, runs a deep valley known from the earliest times as the valley (Hebrew: Gey) of Hinnom, or "Gehinnom." On the southern side of this ravine, opposite Jerusalem, Solomon apparently put up a "high place" (temple) dedicated to Molech (Moloch), the god of the Ammonites, who was pleased by the sacrifice of first-born children, devoured by fire. According to the Books of the Kings and Chronicles, the two rulers Ahaz and Manasseh made their own children "pass through fire"; they also went in for predictions, enchantments, and magic, and employed necromancers and soothsayers and put up idols in the Temple.

It was the great King Josiah (reigned 640–609) who reformed the faith, restoring it to its original purity, which was pleasing to the Lord; he cleared the Temple of the impious images and ordered the valley of Hinnom to be deconsecrated. From that time onward the gorge became the evil-smelling dump for all the city's refuse, a revolting, accursed spot where apparently, among other things, corpses were burned. The name was transformed from Gehinnom to Gehenna, which later came to mean "hell," "place of eternal torment." It is found in the Gospels with this meaning (for instance, in Matt. 5:29, 10:28), as well as in the Koran (Sura 67:8, Sura 89:23–14).

During Josiah's reign a strange occurrence took place whose consequences are still felt today. While the Temple was being repaired, the High Priest Hilkiah discovered an ancient manuscript: "I have found the book of the law..." (II Kings 22:8; II Chron. 34:15). Today the experts believe that this was Deuteronomy, or at least an essential part of it. In Deuteronomy ("The second Law") Moses, instructed directly by God, announced to the Hebrew people most of the 613 commandments which rabbinical exegetes of later times were to find in the text.

The work was attributed to Moses, its great authority was immediately acknowledged, and King Josiah used it as the instrument of a radical religious reform. Seen through our eyes, all these machinations smack of deceit; but we must try to see things through the eyes of an age in which anyone with important things to say attributed them, for greater effect, to some great name of the past. This did not run counter to the ethics of the time. In centuries nearer to our own, pseudepigrapha (writings of one author bearing the name of another, usually ancient and more famous) were to constitute a whole literature.

Josiah's reform was religious, but it also had political aspects. During those

48

years it was easy to predict the fall of Assyrian power, so that the Jewish king was right to gather around him all the forces needed, on various levels, for a possible reconquest of the lands lost from the time of Solomon onward. The reform consisted of a general purification of worship, a return to genuine monotheism, but also in a rigorous centering of worship in the Temple of Jerusalem. From the time of Josiah's reform the religion of Israel took on certain basic features that it still has at the present time. It was Josiah who turned Jerusalem into the uncontested holy city. By now her destiny was clear. Not even total destruction could interrupt an ideal line bringing her, firstly, up to Christ, then to Mohammed and onward, to facts and encounters in the world of today.

After Josiah, royal power fell into the hands of less able or less inspired men. Meanwhile the neo-Babylonian empire was gaining strength with surprising speed. And very soon Jerusalem had to reckon with it.

The siege of Jerusalem lasted one and a half years. Nebuchadnezzar's forces began operations in January 588, and the last resistance of the defenders was overcome in the summer of 587. Oddly enough, Biblical texts are very laconic; the tremendous disaster is summed up in a few lines. The Chaldean forces put any resisters to the sword, "young man or maiden, old man, or him that stooped for age" (II Chron. 36:17), burned the Temple and palaces, and demolished the walls. The survivors were led in slavery to Babylon. Only winegrowers and peasants remained behind, governed by Gedaliah. But after two months Gedaliah was killed as a collaborator, and the last remaining Jews, fearing reprisals, fled to Egypt.

We know that one of the refugees was the prophet Jeremiah, who had uttered desperate, heartfelt prophecies of disaster for his impious country. Tradition (now seriously in doubt) regards him as the author of Lamentations, five poetical compositions. Better than any long prose description, they express the anguish people felt at the fall of a city that must have seemed doubly invincible, defended as it was by both the nature of the place, its fortifications and army, and by the Lord.

But God—offended by the betrayals of the Jews—had changed his love for Jerusalem into hatred. Terrible was his enmity! "Thou hast called as in a solemn day my terrors round about" (Lam. 2:22). "They that be slain with the sword are better than they that be slain with hunger.... The hands of the pitiful women have sodden their own children..." (4:9). Now the enemy passed by and asked, sneering: "Is this the city that men call the perfection of beauty, the joy of the whole earth?" (2:15).

The exile, which lasted a little less than fifty years, was another basic experience in the formation of the Jewish spirit, religion, and civilization. Their common faith acted as a bond among the exiles and enabled them to resist absorption by the enemy and loss of national identity; it was refined and purified by this long lesson of grief and humiliation.

During this period, most probably, when meditation on the past represented a

49

Little mosque

beacon of hope, the Bible began to take shape. Many isolated documents were certainly older, some, such as the song of Deborah, very ancient indeed; but this was a period of redaction and revision which was to lead slowly, about the second century B. C., to the final text and definitive canon of the twenty-four books which make up the Hebrew Bible.

The griefs, frustrations, and anguish of exile also brought about profound changes in the religion of the Israelites. Interest in the past remained very much alive, but the future too began to concern them; if the past offered consolation with its glories, the future gave strength with its hopes. The idea of a Messiah—someone enjoying divine favor who was to come and re-establish freedom and justice in the world—developed, deepened, took on a variety of aspects. A special taste for apocalyptic visions was formed. Ezekiel was one of the first to give accounts of fantastic meetings on the borderline between dream and inspiration. A wild wind breathes through his words; amid phosphorescent clouds, with sudden flashes, there appears a miraculous chariot drawn by four creatures, half man and half beast, hoofed and winged and with the snouts of lions, bulls, and eagles. On this tetralogical vehicle, worthy of a masterpiece by Dürer, stands a sapphire throne holding a human apparition, the "glory of the Lord." Here we are far from the very human God of the Pentateuch or the books of Samuel, who would take patriarchs or kings by the scruff of their necks, and prophets by the throat, commanding, threatening, quick to reproach and revenge but also to pardon and console. If man is to be considered the father rather than the son of God, all is clear: the old Yahweh had emerged from the minds of free shepherds and vigorous warriors; these new and tortuous fantasies consoled a multitude of suffering slaves.

The long stay in Babylon was of crucial importance for the religious future of Israel and, for another reason, the West. Until now the Jews had undergone spiritual influences of various sorts from Egypt and Mesopotamia; but there was a world where a hitherto unknown wealth of thought and mysticism had been flourishing and maturing and about which the Jews knew nothing at all: Persia. Zoroaster—to give a single name to strands that had long been developing in many different minds—had given to Persia a religion in which daring philosophical concepts were mingled with highly mystical imaginings. From Persia Judaism absorbed many ideas that had formerly been foreign to it: for instance, that of the drama of the world seen as a cosmic war between the forces of good and evil, angels and demons; the last judgment, resurrection.... Important elements of the religious heritage of the Christian West have their roots in the religious fire of ancient Persia.

The decline and fall into defeat of the neo-Babylonian empire was as sudden and unexpected as its splendor had been under Nebuchadnezzar. The new rising people this time were the Medes and Persians, with their Indo-European languages and culture, and the new man was Cyrus (Persian: Kurush; Hebrew: Koresh—559–529), founder of the Achaemenid dynasty. After a lucky victory as a young man over the Medes, Cyrus led their soldiers, as well as his own Persians, from victory to victory

50

Arab tomb,
Mamilla Cemetery

across Asia Minor. After conquering the Lydians he arrived at the frontiers of the Greek world; then he turned south, and Babylon was his (538). For the Jews this was freedom; they could go back to Palestine, to the ruins of Jerusalem. Such was the enthusiasm that the second Isaiah greeted Cyrus with hyperbolic praises, actually calling him "the Lord's anointed" or, in Greek, Christ (Isa. 45:1).

After leaving Babylon—where, however, a strong Jewish colony must always have remained—the majority went back to their native land. Here the first thing they did was to set about rebuilding the Temple. The work went on for a good twenty-two years (537–515) because of the lack of means and the continuous subversive opposition of neighboring peoples (Samaritans, Ammonites, Edomites). The new Temple was far more modest than the first: anyone who remembered Solomon's Temple was forced to make a dismal comparison; but at least it had been rebuilt, reopened for worship. And the city, too, was gradually rising up again, with its houses, its walls and gates.

By now absolute independence had been lost. Persian sovereignty, even if exercised benevolently from the distant capitals of Susa and Persepolis, made vain all hopes of military, political, and territorial assertion. Under such circumstances the Jewish people tended to restate their own religious mission. The first century after the exile was one of the most important both in the shaping of the Bible, as a collection of sacred documents, and in the sharpening of religious awareness.

Also, the theological nature of Jewish culture, from exile onward, was reflected in the government of the little country. The period of monarchy was over; the majority had no desire to revive it. Instead, a sort of theocracy prevailed, in which all power was concentrated in the hands of the High Priest. Religious life itself, which in earlier times had been the expression of a creative urge, found its most natural outlet in the progressive organization of its ancestral heritage; ethical principles splintered into minute rules of morals and etiquette; mystical yearning stiffened into ritual; the theophanies experienced on mountain peaks gave way to learned exegeses carried on behind closed doors.

Arab house,
Romema quarter

VIII | MANY BIBLIA INTO ONE BIBLE

Where are those stones—for there must be some, tucked away in some minaret or chapel, under the bed of some Armenian priest, in the back shop of some Arab butcher, or in the foundations of a Talmudic *yeshiva* (seminary)—which one crucial evening in about 450 B.C. witnessed Ezra, who had come back from Babylon at the head of one of the many caravans of Jews returning to Palestine with the blessing of the ruler of Persia, praying fervently in front of the new Temple, at the hour of "the evening sacrifice," on his knees, clothes and mantle torn as a sign of repentance and despair, his hand stretched out toward the Lord, hair and beard in disarray, surrounded by an agitated crowd of the faithful?

What had happened? What was Ezra praying for?

The policy of the Persian kings of the Achaemenid dynasty was completely different from that of the Assyrian and Babylonian rulers. The latter had terrorized their subject peoples with violence and cruelty, and were the inventors of all kinds of tortures (possibly including the cross). Their bas-reliefs are precise and impressively gruesome, showing lion hunts, the destruction of cities, engines of war, impaled prisoners. The Persian kings, though strong in war, followed a more humane and therefore more intelligent policy of peace. Inscriptions of the time tell us that Cyrus was careful to give many subject cities back their images of local gods, which previous rulers had taken to Babylon. Persian policy was liberal toward the Jews too. We have seen how Isaiah greeted Cyrus: "The Lord's anointed." His successors (with the exception of Cambyses II and the usurper Gomates) followed the same line. The Bible gives us a picture of the idyllic relations between Artaxerxes (reigned 465–424) and the Jews. Ezra, "a scribe of the law of the God of heaven" (Ezra 7:12), had been chosen by the Persian king and sent to Jerusalem as the head of all those professing the Jewish religion, in the city and its surroundings.

The vision that the Jewish people had of the universe entailed a particular conception of history. Deuteronomy (26:5–9) gives an excellent summary of the basic points: "A Syrian ready to perish was my father, and he went down into Egypt, and sojourned there with a few, and became there a nation, great, mighty, and populous. And the Egyptians evil entreated us, and afflicted us, and laid upon us hard bondage. And when we cried unto the Lord God of our fathers, the Lord heard our voice, and looked on our affliction, and our labor, and our oppression. And the Lord brought us forth out of Egypt with a mighty hand, and with an outstretched arm, with great terribleness, and with signs and with wonders. And he hath brought us into this place, and given us this land, even a land that floweth with milk and honey." It seems

52

Right
Thalita Kumi building, courtyard

Next four pages
Thalita Kumi building, roof
Thalita Kumi building, roof and courtyard

that this passage was used as a profession of faith, to be recited at the moment of offerings during the Feast of First Fruits (Mishna, Bikk. 3:6). It is also read at the solemn supper on Passover Eve ("Seder").

So the children of Israel were the work of their God; their destiny was in his hands. If Adam had been the first creature on the individual level, Israel could call herself the chosen, elected creature on the collective one. But he was a holy God; so the chosen people must be holy too, lovers of justice. The Lord had descended to Mount Horeb to give Moses the commandments which, if observed, would ensure the holiness of the people. Unfortunately, many, often the entire people, strayed, sinned, worshiped other gods, and forgot justice. Then their God became wrathful and there followed violent death, pestilence, famine, drought, and above all defeat in war. Their enemies were as instruments in his hands: "... the Lord shall set up the adversaries ... against him, and join his enemies together" (Isa. 9:11).

Religious faith thus offered a marvelously simple explanation for the crushing problem of evil, at least on the collective, public level. The people were stained with godlessness, God was offended, there followed misery and suffering.... It took centuries of experience, an immense broadening of horizons, for the fallacy of this premise to become apparent. Furthermore, the oldest Hebrew documents explained individual evil with the same theory. But here it was easier to note how evildoers often prospered while the just suffered. The Book of Job crystallized this greatest of human problems in a poem: how is it possible that a just man should suffer?

The disasters of the fall of Jerusalem and the Babylonian exile were seen within the framework of the cosmic and historical theory. The calamities that had struck innumerable families during these events were interpreted as punishment for godless behavior and injustices perpetrated by fathers and ancestors during the tempestuous centuries of the monarchy—after Solomon and Zedekiah.

If—as no one doubted—all this were true, it must have been equally true that a just government, holiness of worship, and rectitude of conduct ensured, if not glory and wealth, at least peace and quiet. Ezra had come to Jerusalem with these thoughts foremost and with a specific purpose in mind.

That evening he recited a dramatic *nostra culpa* in the square. "For our iniquities have we, our kings, and our priests, been delivered ... to the sword, to captivity ... and to confusion of face..." (Ezra 9:7). But today the Lord has had mercy. Some of us have managed to come back and see Jerusalem again. Now we must pledge ourselves to respect your command, O Lord. And here Ezra quoted a famous passage from Deuteronomy in which the Lord—at the time of the exodus from Egypt—addressed himself to the people, talking of the Promised Land of Canaan, now so near. The peoples among whom you will live, said the Lord, are impure; they practice abominations of all kinds. "Thy daughter thou shalt not give unto his son, nor his daughter shalt thou take unto thy son" (Deut. 7:3).

The return of the Jews from Babylon might in a certain sense be described as a second and lesser exile. The first to re-enter the ruined city were mostly men. Inevit-

53

Mount Zion courtyard,
so-called Tomb of David

ably they married women of the neighboring peoples. Ezra continued his impassioned speech: "Should we again break thy commandments, and join in affinity with the people of these abominations?" Then a member of the crowd stood up, Shechaniah, son of Jehiel, and said: "We have trespassed against our God.... Now therefore let us make a covenant with our God to put away all the wives, and such as are born of them ... be of good courage, and do it" (Ezra 9:14–10:5).

Within a few weeks Operation "Foreign Wives" was completed. In the Book of Ezra there follows a long list of the "culprits."

I have spoken at length about this episode because it reveals much of the intransigent, pedantic, overlogical tone of Ezra's reforms, and also because it illustrates that fanatical spirit of which Jerusalem has been both begetter and victim over the centuries. Holy and accursed city indeed! A city where man, riveted by thoughts of God, forgets man. Think for a moment of those children, sons of the Jews who had come back from Babylon too soon. "Father, Father, why are you sending us away?" "Because God says you are dangerous, you might lead me to false worship." Total apartheid twenty-four centuries *avant la lettre*. And who shall say that the second one, practiced today in the lands under Capricorn, is not descended, in a subtle and roundabout fashion, from the first? (But there was also another school of thought, as the idyllic story of Ruth shows, in which a Moabite woman becomes the ancestor of King David—and the Messiah!)

The work of Ezra—in which the dismissal of the foreign wives was a mere isolated incident—was of prime importance for the rebirth of the Jewish people. Ezra took steps toward renewing the covenant *(berith, testamentum)* between the people and God, he expounded the Torah (Law) to the people in Aramaic—the language which had now become generally used for everyday speech—purified worship according to the most authoritative documents, and set to work to instill religion into all aspects of everyday life. It was during his lifetime that the *synagogue* was born. This word, like *ecclesia,* is Greek, and simply means "congregation"; usually it referred to the community gathered together to pray, to worship, to hear sermons and teachings. It was only later that the words "synagogue" and "church" began to designate the places where these meetings took place.

Also on Ezra's initiative, or about the time he lived, the study of the ancient texts, their redaction and collection together into ever bigger corpuses, was carried on with extraordinary diligence and devotion. Probably this was the time that saw the birth of the idea of a canon, which made one Bible out of so many *biblia*. Under the guidance of Ezra, himself a scribe, a corpus of scribes was formed: men who not only copied out the holy texts but were also able to interpret them and explain them to the people. It seems that such scribes gave public readings at fairs and in market places. The bond between the People and the Book was formed definitively.

One could say that it was under the untiring and scrupulous guidance of Ezra that real Judaism was born, a religion markedly different from that of heroic theophanies and miracles. In the last analysis, many phenomena of the religious life that also characterize the two religions born of Judaism stem from Ezra. For instance, the idea of a weekly meeting to worship, pray, and teach; the form of such meetings (prayers, readings, songs); the idea of a scriptural canon. The New Covenant (Testament) and the Koran would be inconceivable without the Bible as ancestor.

Together with Ezra, or at least during the same period, Nehemiah too was sent to Jerusalem by the Persian king, as governor. The work of the two men was decisive but complementary. Ezra presided over the religious rebirth, Nehemiah over the material rebuilding of the city. As soon as he arrived from Persia, secretly, at dead of night, Nehemiah made a tour of inspection of the walls. "And I went out by night by the gate of the valley, even before the dragon well, and to the dung port, and viewed the walls of Jerusalem, which were broken down.... Then I went on to the gate of the fountain, and to the king's pool" (Neh. 2:13–14). As soon as he could, Nehemiah gathered together those who had returned to Jerusalem and told them of his plan to rebuild the walls. All responded enthusiastically.

The work was very difficult. There was a dearth of materials, and stones had to be salvaged from the old fortifications and palaces. Furthermore, it all had to be done in secret, not so much because of the Persian authorities, who were willing to turn a blind eye, as because of the neighboring peoples, particularly those of Samaria, who emphatically did not want a strong and perhaps aggressive Jerusalem to rise up once again. At night a vigilant watch was kept; by day the Jews worked like beavers "and with the other hand held a weapon" (Neh. 4:17). Many of the Jews themselves regarded Nehemiah as an unrealistic visionary and did not wish to follow him in his frenetic labors. Others plotted to prevent him. But Nehemiah triumphed: after about fifty-two days Jerusalem had her encircling walls and was a real city once again.

IX | LEARNED AND DISENCHANTED TIMES

Jerusalem, with Judaea, remained under the rule of the Persian kings for more than two centuries. We know very little of this period. When the name of the city reappears in history Alexander the Great (356–323) was already on the scene. The account of a visit of his to the holy hill of Zion is apparently legendary, for in reality the Greek conqueror must have followed the coastal route, both in his lightning descent upon Egypt and on his way back. Jerusalem automatically became part of his realm when he succeeded to Cyrus the Younger and the Achaemenid kings.

From the point of view of cultural influences, three successive periods can be seen in the history of Jerusalem. From David's conquest to the arrival of Alexander, for about seven centuries, her relations were almost exclusively with countries with Semitic traditions: Egypt, Mesopotamia, Syria, the kingdoms of Damascus, the city-states of Phoenicia. The more one studies the history of these countries, in either written or archaelogical documents, the more one is struck by how close and active the exchanges were with such people, within the field of ideas, worship, and art.

Beginning with Alexander and continuing with his successors there was a long period—almost a thousand years—in which Jerusalem was linked to the West, particularly to Greece, and during which it underwent—variously, subtly, deeply—the influence first of the Hellenistic civilization, then of the Greco-Roman, and lastly of the Byzantine. In 636 B.C. a third period started, which lasted until the threshold of our times, in which Jerusalem, except for the interlude of her Crusader masters, was to live once more within the orbit of Eastern civilization.

The events of these centuries were reviewed by the prophet Daniel in the form of apocalyptic visions, in which heaven and earth, cosmos and history, eschatology and symbolism came together in fantastic counterpoint. First we are presented with a colossal statue, seen in a dream by King Nebuchadnezzar, with a head of gold, breast and arms of silver, belly and thighs of brass, legs of iron, feet of iron mixed with clay (Dan. 2:32). This was the traditional depiction of the ages of history symbolized by successive metals, each baser than the last. The various metals represented the neo-Babylonians, the Medes, the Persians, the Greeks of Alexander, the Diadochi. Suddenly a stone breaks off from a mountain, shattering the statue (Dan. 2:45)—a symbol of the kingdom of heaven, which will "never be destroyed."

In another vision, that born "of the head" of Daniel himself (Dan. 7:1), four enormous beasts "came up from the sea": a lion (the Babylonians), a fierce bear devouring a meal of ribs (the Medes), a leopard with the wings of a fowl (the Persians), a monster "dreadful and terrible, and strong exceedingly," with teeth of iron and ten

56

Memorial candles
so-called Tomb of David

horns on its head (Alexander and his Diadochi). Among the ten horns there sprouted one with human eyes and a mouth "speaking great things" (7:8): Antiochus IV Epiphanes.

Such horrendous fantasies, if they found place in the Biblical canons, must have corresponded broadly to the tastes and expectations of the public. It would be unfair to characterize this miraculous and simple-minded manner of interpreting history as typically Jewish and the deep search for human motives of a Thucydides, or the honest reporting of a Xenophon, as typically Hellenic. The Jews knew how to write marvelous history when they wanted to: the account of the succession of David (II Sam. 13–20 and I Kings 1–2) has been described repeatedly as a masterpiece of ancient historiography. But with the passing of time and the declining of earthly fortunes, with the development of the messianic hopes which would lead to the replacing of the present world order, irremediably rotten and corrupt, by a new one, there was a progressive loss of contact with reality; dreams and fantasies, epiphany and demiurgy became the normal forms of escape. We are moving toward learned and disenchanted times, similar to our own, in which the mature society of the Mediterranean countries, unified by now, was to search for a secret peace of mind in the worship of Isis and Adonis, Ishtar and Tammuz, Cybele, Mithra, and lastly Christ, in which every Jewish synagogue was to be the center of a large number of sympathizers, uncircumcised theists, when the learned and the sophisticated turned to neo-Platonism, Gnosticism, or declared themselves disciples of Pythagoras. Somehow the same process seems to have taken place in India. Just for the fun of it one might compare certain successive stages in Hebrew literature—Genesis, Chronicles, Prophets, Apocalypse, and Cabala—with others farther east: Veda, Upanishads, Brahmana, Purana, and Tantra.

On the early death of Alexander (323) the newly born empire fell apart. After a struggle among his generals which lasted over forty years, stability returned and Jerusalem found itself under the rule of Ptolemy, sovereign of Egypt. An odd fact: Ptolemy entered Jerusalem for the first time (320) on a Saturday, holy day of rest when soldiers could not take up arms. Luckily for Jerusalem, the rule of the Ptolemies was the most stable of all the various regimes inheriting Alexander's empire. Ostensibly Jerusalem was protected by a garrison faithful to a distant king of Greek extraction, but the Jews (provided they paid their taxes) enjoyed considerable autonomy under the responsibility of the High Priest. His position was not hereditary; he was chosen from among the sons of a limited number of families. Jerusalem's autonomy is attested by the fact that it had its own local coinage.

Relations between Egypt and Judaea must have been friendly for a long time. Gradually an important Jewish community grew up in Alexandria, where Greek finally tended to be spoken more than Aramaic. It was at Alexandria, about 250 B.C., that it was decided to translate the Bible into Greek. Legend says that there were seventy translators (hence the "Septuagint" version), that they worked for seventy-two days, each on his own; at the end they had seventy identical versions, the tangible

Old houses,
Mount Zion

proof of divine inspiration. The remains of the Alexandria synagogue are apparently the oldest hitherto discovered.

The Ptolemaic peace lasted barely a century. The Seleucid kings of Syria, who were the most restless and ambitious of Alexander's successors, had long dreamed of broadening the bounds of their own kingdom. Antiochus III (the Great) aspired to rebuild Alexander's empire, and he would perhaps have managed to do so if he had not found himself faced with the new Mediterranean power, Rome. The Panhellenic dream was perforce forgotten, and in the meantime Jerusalem had been taken. The successors of Antiochus III (died 187 B.C.) inherited a difficult position; to finance themselves they had the idea of seizing the treasures of the numerous temples in their own territories. Since there were no banks in those days, temples often served as public safes; this happened in Jerusalem as elsewhere.

But much harder times were in the offing. The moment of the eleventh horn of Daniel's monster had come: that of Antiochus IV Epiphanes (reigned 175–163 B.C.) —God manifest. Judgment of historical figures differs according to one's point of view: Genghis Khan is a hero in traditional Chinese historiography, a scourge in the Russian, in the modern Mongol a loathed imperialist who stripped the country of young lives to satisfy personal ambition. Antiochus IV observed through Hellenic (Polybius) or Hellenizing (Flavius Josephus) eyes was an ambitious sovereign, afflicted with a certain *folie de grandeur,* but basically intent on the sacred task of spreading the light and civilization of the Greek spirit among those luckless enough to be born barbarians. But seen through Jewish eyes, he was the sinful branch of an accursed house, a loathed tyrant, the incarnation of the forces of evil hostile to God. It has been said that the very conception of Antichrist was fostered by the image that Antiochus Epiphanes left in the minds of the Jews of his time.

What did Antiochus do that was so terrible? His dominions were vast, and were populated by a variety of peoples; many languages were spoken in them, many gods worshiped. It was logical to attempt somehow to unify such divergent and mutually hostile forces. This union was to be produced by means of the Greek language, the civilization of Hellas, the pagan religion. To this end Antiochus claimed for himself absolute authority over all other religions, over all temples and their riches. It should, furthermore, have been possible to reach some sort of agreement: the Hellenic concept of life was not only enlightened, reasonable, humane, but also hospitable; it opened its arms eagerly to foreign cults, willing to concede a certain degree of compromise. Judaism, in its Temple, in the stronghold of Jerusalem, refused all compromise; it was like a rock sticking out of an otherwise absolutely level country. In a similar way, Antiochus' successors, the Romans, would be confronted by the Christians, part heirs of the Judaic tradition.

As always happens to a society in which there is strong external pressure, the Jews split into two groups: one the conservatives, advocating resistance to the bitter end, another the philhellenes, prepared for compromises. For some years Antiochus could count on the Hellenizers—the very names of the High Priests (Jason, Menelaus)

58

tell us more than many a long discourse—and Jerusalem must have begun to look like one of the innumerable cities of a world now homogeneous from Alexandria to Cyrene, from Syracuse to Corinth. A gymnasium was built, where youths met for athletic competitions in the Greek fashion, i.e., naked, and Antiochus himself went up to Jerusalem like a mythical hero, to be received by the jubilant crowd "by torch-light" (II Mac. 4:22).

Such an idyl could not last long. There came a moment when Antiochus felt that the city was turning against him. He leaped down from the north "like a wild beast" (II Mac. 5:11), took Jerusalem by force, and let loose his own soldiers inside the walls. There followed one of those horrendous massacres so common in the tortured history of the holy city: "Then there was killing of young and old, destruction of boys, women, and children, and slaughter of virgins and infants" (II Mac. 5:13). The author of the Second Book of the Maccabees talks of forty thousand dead and forty thousand carried off to be sold in slavery. This may be an exaggeration, but it was plainly a most ferocious act of vengeance. Naturally, the Temple was sacked of its treasures, and Antiochus, it was said, returned to his capital with eighteen hundred talents (about $22.5 million).

To complete submission to the king's will, observance of the Mosaic law was forbidden, and pagan cults were introduced in the Temple. A statue of Olympian Zeus had the place of honor, and during the Dionysiac festivals "the Jews were compelled to walk in the procession in honor of Dionysus, wearing wreaths of ivy" (II Mac. 6:7). As always happens when it is a question of beliefs, imposition and resistance exacerbate one another. Two poor women who had dared to circumcise their sons were led in procession through the city ("their children at their breast") and then hurled from the top of the walls. Other unfortunates, wanting to observe the Sabbath in a cave, were discovered and burned alive. It was an age of martyrs. The old Eleazar, "one of the foremost of the law," was beaten to death for having refused to eat pork. An even more horrific end awaited the famous seven brothers, and their mother, for the same reason (II Mac. 7).

The Greeks and their king were hated for such excesses. Peaceful Hellenization might perhaps have had some success; imposed with such brutish heavy-handedness, it could have only one outcome: revolt.

The first to hoist the banner of revolt (167 B.C.) was a certain Mattathias of Modin, father of five sons. When Syrian officials arrived in his little village, to impose apostasy and make the Jews carry out sacrifices forbidden by Mosaic law, Mattathias and his family refused. Furthermore, "inflamed with zeal," he slew a fellow Jew preparing a sacrifice in accordance with the king's command, as well as a Syrian functionary, pulled down the altar, then fled into the mountains with his sons. "Whosoever is zealous of the law, and maintaineth the covenant, let him follow me" (I Mac. 2:27) was the battle cry. Within a short time the heroic actions of the small group, joined by many enemies of the foreign domination, gained Mattathias and his sons the name that soon became famous: *makkabah,* hammer (and history refers to

59

them as the Maccabees). It was a decidely popular movement, and immensely successful. When Mattathias died he was succeeded by his third son, Judas, who led the rebels from victory to victory and finally occupied Jerusalem (165 B.C.). The Temple was promptly purified, and the event is still celebrated every year at the feast called Hanukkah—"dedication"—which has particular significance and importance in Israel today.

Officially Judas had no special job; in reality he found himself the ruler of a new state and, as such, concluded various alliances. An elementary political principle—"my enemy's enemy is my friend"—led him to ally himself with the new and powerful adversary of the Greeks, with Rome.

When peoples know each other only at a distance, they are liable to a touching enthusiasm. For Europe, the China of the eighteenth century was the utopian land of wisdom, of all civic virtue, justice, and moderation. A hundred years later, distances had shrunk, judgments were reversed: Europeans saw China as a country of presumptuous peasants, while the Chinese saw Europe as the continent of red-haired "devils." In the First Book of the Maccabees any mention of the Romans amounts to a string of praises: the Romans are strong, they have conquered such and such a king, Antiochus the Great hoped to foil them with a hundred and twenty elephants but was promptly dealt with, the Greeks had the worst of it. "Yet for all this none of them wore a crown, or was clothed in purple, to be magnified thereby; moreover they had made for themselves a senate house, wherein three hundred and twenty men sat in council daily, consulting always for the people, to the end they might be well ordered" (I Mac. 8:14). It is amazing to think that, a few generations later, Jews and Romans were to be locked in loathing and fight a battle to the death.

Judas soon lost his life in battle. He was succeeded by his brother Jonathan (ruled 162–142), who renewed the alliance with the Romans and tried to conclude another with Sparta. Apparently the Spartans had sent a letter to the High Priest of Jerusalem greeting the Jews as brothers in Abraham. The form of the letter, if not the substance, is plainly the work of a late revision. Jonathan was the first of the Maccabees to unite the functions of High Priest with those of military and civil leader—strategist and governor. Judaea's independence now existed not only *de facto* but actually *de jure,* with the explicit recognition of the king of Syria. The last of the Maccabees to occupy the position of first citizen was Simon (ruled 142–135), on whom, out of gratitude, his followers wished to bestow hereditary rights to the High Priesthood and princedom.

With the death of the last of the three brothers the name "Maccabees" passed into history. Simon was followed by John Hyrcanus (ruled 135–104), and beginning with him the dynasty was referred to as that of the Hasmoneans, after a distant ancestor. The long reign of John Hyrcanus had some stormy moments. At one stage Antiochus VII of Syria besieged Jerusalem, but then recalled his troops after payment of a heavy tribute. Under John Hyrcanus, the Jewish state made important internal progress and extended its borders in several directions.

60

It is interesting to remember that John Hyrcanus, in one of his campaigns, conquered the territory of the Idumaeans (to the south of Palestine), declaring that he would allow this people to keep their own hereditary lands if they were circumcised and respected the law of Moses. Flavius Josephus tells us that the Idumaeans, strongly attacked on their own ground, let themselves be circumcised, accepting the Jewish way of life: "And from that day onward they were always considered Jewish, to all intents and purposes" (Ant. XIII 9:1). The same happened with certain peoples who lived in the north, on the borders of the Lebanon, conquered and Judaized (104–103) by Aristobulus I. This new Jewish state reached its maximum size during the reign (103–76) of Alexander Jannaeus, the first of the Hasmoneans to declare himself not only High Priest but also king. The kingdom of the Hasmoneans was not much smaller, territorially, than that of David and Solomon, eight centuries before.

One might imagine this to have been a period of prosperity and concord. But quite the opposite was true: on the one hand the continuous wars, although they extended the borders of the kingdom, began to weigh on the people, and on the other the new monarchy became increasingly unpopular. At first the revolt of the Maccabees had been a spontaneous religious movement, popular in character, but after the establishment of the Hasmonean dynasty the individual kings had given proof of overtly political and worldly ambitions. Furthermore, many citizens were unwilling to recognize, or simply did not recognize, the right of the Hasmoneans to the High Priesthood. According to a very ancient tradition, only members of certain families could aspire to this position.

So as time passed a curious reversal of values and camps had occurred. The traditionalists, represented mainly by the Pharisees, who had sided with Mattathias and his sons, who had enabled them to beat the Syrian Greeks and to free Judaea, were now the king's fiercest and most implacable enemies; while on the king's side were the Temple officials, the Sadducees, the very men whom the sovereign's ancestors had fought so fiercely.

For years the country was in a state of chaos. At one point Alexander Jannaeus managed to seize about eight hundred rebels, whom he took prisoner to Jerusalem. Here, according to the historian Flavius Josephus, while the king was celebrating the event with his concubines in the sight of the whole city, he had them crucified; furthermore, while his victims were still alive he had their wives and children slaughtered in front of their eyes (Ant. XIII 14:2).

By now the rift between rulers and people had become irreparable. After the death of Alexander Jannaeus, his wife Alexandra managed to reign for about ten years (76–67 B.C.), wisely relying on the Pharisees for support and dividing power with her son Hyrcanus II, who had the position of High Priest. When Alexandra died Hyrcanus II was faced with his brother Aristobulus as a rival, and the country was plunged into civil war once again. The Romans, who under Pompey were based in Syria, where they were destroying what remained of the power of the Seleucids, profited from the confusion.

61

Gatepost, Mahaneh Yehuda quarter

The two brothers turned to Pompey as arbiter of their dispute, but did not seem satisfied with his answer. Pompey then decided to occupy Jerusalem, where Aristobulus's faction was entrenched in the Temple. Once again the ancient walls were besieged—and once again the besiegers were successful, according to Flavius Josephus, because the Jews did not fight on the Sabbath. The law allowed for defense against a regular attack on the Sabbath, but it did not countenance action against an enemy intent on its own business. The Romans took advantage of the hours of calm to erect glacises and prepare the engines of siege. After three months the besieged surrendered; the Romans, together with Hyrcanus's supporters, invaded the city. There followed another of those massacres witnessed only too often by the patient stones of the city: twelve thousand Jews were slaughtered while innumerable desperate men threw themselves from the bastions or set fire to their houses. Pompey and his officers entered the Temple and set foot in the Holy of Holies, open only once a year to the High Priest. The Temple was full of treasures, including two thousand talents ($25 million) in offerings, which Pompey, "because of his high esteem for religion," did not touch. Later, however, the Romans imposed a huge tax of at least ten thousand talents on the Jews.

Jerusalem and its territory had now lost all independence; Rome had put them among its tributary states. Hyrcanus was appointed High Priest and ethnarch of the Jews (he therefore had no royal or territorial power) while the Idumaean Antipater was made governor. Aristobulus, taken prisoner in the war, was made to walk in front of the consular chariot in the triumph that Rome offered Pompey on his return home (61 B.C.). Many other prisoners marched in the same triumphal procession; with time, these men and women joined the blossoming Jewish community in Rome.

X | IN THE SQUARE OF THE SANCTIFIED

MOON

Tall, strangely forbidding houses of light stone, enigmatic windows through which no one ever looks, or which frame the faces of motionless old women, like stony statues; arches and stairways leading to mysterious destinations, a far-off sky, silence, wind, dust, sun: this is Mea Shearim, the Orthodox Jewish quarter in Jerusalem.

It is not very old. It dates back to the second half of the nineteenth century, when important groups of Jews began to go back to Palestine, encouraged and often assisted by Moses Montefiore. At that time they lived only inside the walled city, as the countryside was unsafe; this is why many of the houses in Mea Shearim look rather like fortresses, with big courtyards protected by great doorways and strongly barred windows. The name, which means "a hundredfold," apparently comes from a phrase in the Biblical text read on the day the quarter was founded (Gen. 26:12): "Then Isaac sowed in that land, and received in the same year an hundredfold, and the Lord blessed him." Others, however, say that it can mean "the hundred gates," referring to the many courtyard entrances.

It was the Sabbath. There were no vehicles around, because it would be a sin to turn on an engine—sparks, therefore fire; no fire on the Sabbath. Cars sleep at the roadside like slumped camels. Powerful cars, not neglected—on the contrary, well kept up, but without frills or luxurious fittings.

The streets were filled with men, women, and children coming back from the Wall, going to synagogue or returning from it. I saw patriarchs with flowing white beards, dressed in long, dark coats of expensive materials and varying shapes, with their big round fur hats *(shtreimel)*, like haloes for hyperborean saints. I saw bespectacled young men dressed in dark clothes, with nascent beards, walking along with an air of seriousness that was strangely proud and humble at the same time. There were groups of children already bearing the indelible stamp of their upbringing, with their shorts down to their knees, their little skullcaps perched on their heads, and their first inches of side curls down their cheeks.

The women were easily recognizable: their dress, except for the colors, was like a novice's garb. They wore dresses with wide sleeves, neat and colorful, but ageless and styleless; they wore thick stockings, usually black, and big kerchiefs on their heads which often—if they were married—covered shaven skulls. Long hair is one of the many frivolities that is often scorned in Orthodox families.

Whole families were out walking. It was strange: here one saw just the opposite of what one sees elsewhere. Usually, women are more conservative than men. In Turkey, Afghanistan, India, Japan, you often see the husband walk ahead wearing

63

Ethiopian quarter

jacket and trousers, followed by his wife with a veil or burka over her face, in sandals and sari, or obi and kimono, tabi and zori on her feet. In Mea Shearim, if one of a couple rejects the costume of their ancestors, it is more often the woman. Here was a family with the husband, a fine man of about forty, impeccably dressed in the traditional manner, the headgear of the just, while the woman has rebelled, has long hair (though it might be a wig!), and is wearing a dress which, without having exactly a miniskirt, is nonetheless fairly normal female attire.

Many men were wearing white wool shawls with black or blue stripes (tallith) on their shoulders, and carrying books under their arms. The shawl, for reasons of ritual and specifications made in the law, must be of the purest wool. I was told that the quarter had a modern laboratory, especially equipped, where any cloth sample could instantly be analyzed, if it did not contravene the Biblical prohibition: "... nor shall there come upon you a garment of cloth made of two kinds of stuff" (Lev. 19:19).

The men with their shawls were coming or going from one of the many synagogues of the district. Here and there snatches of prayer could be heard, intoned rhythmically in chorus. To be valid, prayers must be recited by at least ten male people at once (minyan), one of the basic facts which helps to explain the Jewish sense of group, the feeling for community life; and a fact which also helps one to understand the kibbutz phenomenon. You pray together, live together, work together.

There are a number of synagogues in the quarter, and study houses (Beth-midrash), religious schools (heder), Talmudic seminaries (yeshivot). The buildings are completely unadorned: houses just like any others, though with bigger rooms, sometimes, so that people can gather there. An almost brutally functional sense predominates. Everything that could distract from the single thought—God and his Word—is omitted, avoided. Beauty? Not bad in itself, in theory, but in practice why waste time on it? Why think of flowers, decorations? Few things are essential to life, and one should manage with only them. In any case, anyone really intending conscientously to follow the 613 commandments of the law (248 positive and 365 negative) has little time left for anything else; his days and nights are filled with "things to do".... This is why one may well say that traditional Judaism is more concerned with orthopraxy than with orthodoxy. Follow the rules scrupulously, then mind and soul will be free to meet the Lord in a hundred different ways.

The Orthodox of Mea Shearim belong to many different schools, different groups. Theoretically there should be a gulf between the mystically inclined Hasidim and the strictly Orthodox rabbis. The original Hasidim were members of a movement of protest, of mystical revival, born of the experience of the Cabala, but which then developed in opposition to it and its hermeticism. The founder of modern Hasidism was Baal Shem Tob (the Master of the Divine Name), who lived in Poland during the eighteenth century (died 1760). The Hasidim preach a doctrine transcending the written word, a return to nature, to clarity of speech, to intuition, divine madness, joy. In a sense one could draw a parallel between Hasidic Judaism and Zen Buddhism.

64

I think a Hasid would fully agree with the famous words of Hui-Neng: "There is a special tradition outside the scriptures. Do not attach importance to documents or books; fulfill your nature and become Buddha."

Unfortunately, I am told, even the Hasidim finally yielded to an almost irresistible tendency in Judaism, that of making laws, of transforming life into a mathematical system of symbols and rites, of freezing even spontaneity into tables, of formalizing even the rejection of form. Thus—I repeat, so I am told, for it is difficult to penetrate this closed, suspicious world—if the various groups are based on different theoretical approaches to scripture, in practice their rules appear to be fairly similar.

I walked past some of the synagogues; here is the Yeshiva Talmud Torah Mea Shearim, frequented as a seminary by crowds of boys; then there are the Hasidic ones, the Ohel Itzhak ("Tent of Isaac") and the Rab Araleh. Lastly there are tribal or communal synagogues, those of the Yemenites, the Persians.

The synagogue Beit Yosse ("House of Joseph") belongs to the most extreme sect of Mea Shearim, that known as the sect of the Naturey Karta ("Protectors of the City," i.e., of Jerusalem; in reality, the "Guardians of Orthodoxy"). There are about four thousand of these sectarians, and they abide by the strictest rabbinical injunctions and refuse to recognize the secular state of Israel. This state, if it were really to come into existence, could only be the work of the Messiah, hence their continual dogged boycotting of all that represents the state as it is at present, their refusal to send their children to its schools, to allow them to do military service, to perform any act that would imply recognition of a policy regarded as immoral, an obstacle to the coming of the Messiah.

In a state with such strong religious roots, their position is indeed neither negligible nor ridiculous. In fact they manage to exert a sort of moral blackmail over many other less ardent believers. It is largely owing to their pressure that the state of Israel has no provision for civil marriage.

This idealistic and fanatical tension finds expression in a variety of writings on the walls: they are in Hebrew, of course, but a young man walking with me explains them eagerly. Here are a few signs made with just such a brush as we would use to write "Up with Mao" or "Mary is lovely," but which say: "Don't read the newspapers, they are all impure!" Printed manifestoes exhort young women to dress modestly, or protest against the use of cars on the Sabbath.

In certain writings one notes a painful incompatibility with modern life. Some of the 613 commandments are certainly no longer relevant (for example, "You shall not sacrifice your own sons to Moloch!"). But many of the thirty-nine Sabbath prohibitions may seem extreme—among them, the prohibiting of lighting fires, therefore of producing sparks, therefore of running cars or trains. But there are more serious matters. Some passages of the law can be interpreted as prohibiting the dissection of corpses, hence the continual protests against the use of corpses in universities and hospitals. A large scrawl reads: "No more dissections. We don't want our dead profaned! So-and-so [and there follows the name of a well-known

65

House, Nahlat Shiv'ah

Israeli physician] is worse than Hitler!" The polemic even reached Parliament. In contrast, the University of Jerusalem announced:

> Hadassah Medical Organisation Ein Karem and The Hebrew University, Medical School, Jerusalem, pay tribute to the memory of X, who died on..., having bequeathed his body to the advancement of Science.

A positive war cry of romantic and committed secularism!

On the other hand, in the little square of Kiddush Levannah ("Sanctification of the New Moon") there is a large inscription, six feet high and three wide. This is a gentle, poetic prayer to God, thanking him for having put the new moon in the sky again. It is recited each month, as soon as the faintest sliver of new moon can be seen, and every night until the moon becomes full. In the olden days the nomads were alarmed every time the star of night seemed to sicken and die. Its return was a miracle, and hence the spontaneous thanks offered to God.

The world of the Orthodox of Mea Shearim is a strange world, absurd in a sense, sometimes almost sublime; often odd to the point of madness; probably quite unbearable for those not born into it. How do these people live? What do they want? I asked my companion. Some of them have small businesses, many receive offerings from other less ardent faithful, living abroad perhaps and hoping to store up treasure in the coffers of heaven.... I felt that the clamorous victory in the 1967 war was considered a miracle here, "due partly to our prayers," exclaims a bearded old man who looks like Tolstoy. It was the same theory I had heard put forward by the lamas of Tibet, and indeed by certain Catholic nuns: prayer as a sort of spiritual fuel of the world, charging the batteries of divine grace.

Will things change? I don't think so. It is a self-perpetuating world. The young are educated in the local schools, where they learn only what is approved by the council of elders. Every contact with the "others" is considered improper, dangerous, a source of sin.

Another day: a working day. We went in to visit a school, six or seven classrooms looking onto a big balcony. They were bleak rooms, bare, dark, the medieval antithesis of a modern classroom; I saw worn, yellowish benches. In the first room were ten to twelve children, no more than three or four years old, endlessly repeating, aloud, passages from the Torah read by a master who was young, but bearded and bespectacled and wearing his hat. In nearby classrooms slightly older children were reading, as well as reciting aloud. This total immersion in the Torah, the Mosaic law, lasts from infancy to adulthood.

My companion told me about a young acquaintance of his in this quarter, who read in a magazine of certain discoveries concerning "fossils dating back thirty million years." Worried, he went to his master for explanations. He was solemnly scolded and punished. "The world is exactly five thousand seven hundred and twenty-nine years old," he was told. "Do you think you know more than the holy scriptures?"

66

Flight of steps,
Yemin Moshe

My companion, while criticizing many aspects of this enclosed horizon, this self-perpetuating ghetto re-created as it were out of nostalgia, had nonetheless undergone the subtle fascination of mysticism. Like people in Catholic countries who rail against priests, or the Vatican hierarchy, but then fall down in ecstasy before a wonder-working priest. He insisted on saying to me: "Believe me, they're happy. They have no worries. They study, read, meditate, pray. They are awaiting the Messiah with joy." Furthermore, he added: "Don't worry about them, they're certain they're the chosen among a chosen people!"

For me this remark, made almost jokingly, was like a lamp illuminating a myriad of nocturnal suspicions. That was it! Here was the explanation of the transparent but unrendable veil put up between them and the "ordinary man." Rarely, though I have traveled a great deal, have I encountered more "alien" human beings, men less accessible to any approach. Take Tibetan lamas, Indian sadhus, Japanese kamikazes. In these men—certainly very different from ourselves—a particular faith, a subtle magic, an almost insane fanaticism may stretch the fabric of ordinary humanity to the breaking point; yet in each case, I remember, a smile, a word, a gesture could bridge the gap. Not here; here was a yawning rift, an unfordable abyss. It really was like suddenly coming across Martians just out of their spacecraft after having landed silently on the village green. Nor did the myth of their happiness persuade me. Can one really be happy locked up so rigidly in a frequently irate fanaticism?

Another Sabbath: I saw patriarchs of infinite dignity coming down a small stairway, striped shawls over their shoulders, their long coats like those of apothecaries in Flemish paintings, and their big hats like those of Polish noblemen. I tried to photograph them and instantly regretted it. The patriarchs snarled, ran forward shrieking, swearing, their mouths, so shortly before pursed in the mild pronouncing of sacred formulae, now opened and closed; I saw yellowish teeth, throats full of spit and foam, eyes expressing hatred and disgust. Young people ran to the side of the old, prepared to pick up stones.

I no longer believed in the myth of their happiness. I have seen happy people; they are different. Serene, gentle, open. In any case, it is clear, one can't really be happy while harboring in one's heart the pride of someone who regards himself as special, better than others, chosen by God: nursing the ambition to deserve this state by following a thorny path which separates him in many ways, almost all of them important, from the rest of the world.

Finally, how can you be happy when cunning is raised to the level of a virtue and hypocrisy to a method? To observe the 613 commandments and yet not lose any advantages, the most ingenious subterfuges have been invented. Married women shave their heads? Fine, but no commandment prohibits them from wearing other people's hair, so here are your wigs! Men mustn't draw metal blades over their faces? They can use plastic ones, electric razors, or even depilatory creams! And so on in dozens of cases.

Let us leave Mea Shearim. In a few minutes we are at the other end of Jerusalem,

67

House, Mishkenot quarter

on the hills with the National Museum, the Hebrew University, and Parliament. If in Mea Shearim we were immersed in a fossilized Pentateuch, here we are projected toward the future. Light, brightness, gaiety, flowers, youth, a world both free and committed, charming and serious; the absolute, final antithesis of the other faces of Jerusalem—so near and yet so far.

68

XI | A TEMPLE REBUILT

The Hasmonean dynasty met its downfall after vain attempts to regain power; the rising star was now that of Antipater, a past master in currying favor with the Romans. When he died he was succeeded by his son Herod, young but full of ambitions and determined to realize them by any means available. Like his father, Herod knew how to manage the Romans. Cornered by the plots of the last Hasmoneans, he fled to Egypt (and Cleopatra) and then to Rome. Here, with the support of Antony and Augustus, he was able to plan so cleverly, to pave his way with such splendid gifts, that in less than a week the senate named him king of Judaea.

At this point Herod was king only on paper—or rather on parchment. Now he had to reconquer Judaea. The *de facto* ruler in Jerusalem was Antigonus, the last of the Hasmoneans, who had managed to take the city with the support of the Parthians; the rest of the country was overrun by bands of partisans. It took three years of guerrilla warfare—of which Flavius Josephus has reported many ferocious episodes—to establish peace. Finally, only Jerusalem remained to be conquered. Once again high glacises were prepared for the machines, and hunger struck again within the walls. After five months Herod's forces—supported by Romans from the provinces of Syria—managed to break through the walls, near the Temple. Herod had wanted only to enter "his" capital and drive out Antigonus, without doing too much harm to a people he knew he was going to have to govern, but the soldiers, maddened by so many months of resistance and anticipation, launched into a brutal massacre. "Multitudes were slaughtered in the narrow streets while seeking refuge in their houses or fleeing toward the sanctuary. There was no pity for infancy or old age, nor for women in their weakness." The soldiers hacked at everyone within their reach. Antigonus, in terror, went to throw himself at the feet of the governor of Syria, who welcomed him with a chilling smile and called him by the female version of his name: Antigone.

Herod is a complex figure, of strong contrasts. A skillful administrator and great builder on the one hand, he was also violent, suspicious, and cruel: he could be irresistibly entertaining when the occasion called for it, cultivated useful friendships, and turned everything to his own advantage. Basically he always remained the provincial who has made good, who was fascinated by the aristocracy, in his case, the Hasmoneans, by a great religion into which he was only just accepted (Judaism), and by the world's most powerful men—Antony, then Augustus.

Once the kingdom was his *de jure* and *de facto,* Herod devoted himself for many years to works of peace, with the exceptions of a few martial intervals. His family

Off Agrippa's road

life, however, brought him continual torment and tragedy. Partly to ingratiate himself with the Jews and partly because she must have been a women of singular fascination, Herod married Mariamne, daughter of Hyrcanus II. This link with the last Hasmonean princess made him the relative by marriage of many aristocrats who could have become his rivals. Mariamne's seventeen-year-old brother, Aristobulus, was appointed High Priest, and Herod soon became jealous of the enthusiasm the young man aroused in the crowd during the festive ceremonies. With diabolical gentleness he had him drowned. Later Hyrcanus appeared tempted to take part in a plot; Herod did away with him too. Then came the turn of Mariamne, suspected of adultery and conspiracy. Finally Mariamne's mother and a whole group of descendants of the Hasmonean house were also put to death. Only when Herod knew that he had destroyed the very roots of the family that might in some way have harmed him, did he feel safe. But his last years were stained by other family crimes. Herod was offended by the success of the sons he had had by Mariamne, who had Hasmonean blood; he imagined that the young men wanted to remove him from power and could not rest until they had been strangled. The last was Antipater, his father's favorite. It is possible that Antipater had really thought of hastening his father's death; he was promptly imprisoned and then, with the permission of the Roman authorities, done away with. Just four days later Herod died (4 B.C.).

The affairs of Herod and his family remind one of some of the great families of the Italian Renaissance—the Borgias, the Malatestas—in which love, murder, poison, suspicion, and vengeance intermingle against a background of palaces, processions, wars, festivities, and boundless wealth. And Herod, just like a Renaissance lord, while giving orders to his personal guerrillas to strangle relatives, or intimidating law courts to extort death sentences on a wife, was also building amphitheaters and hippodromes, embellishing his own capital and the provincial cities, constructing fortresses, keeping the peace, and administering his kingdom with skill and indeed wisdom.

"Of the rulers of antiquity," says Stewart Perowne, "it was Herod who devoted himself with the greatest passion to building—possibly only the Emperor Hadrian surpassed him."

Apart from his activities in the capital, he founded the city and port of Caesarea, with its lavish marble buildings, whose remains sparkle even today in the Mediterranean sun. He founded new colonies, where the grudging land of the mountains of Judaea permitted it—Sebaste in Samaria, Antipatris, and others—provided public buildings for Tripoli, Damascus, Antioch, Byblos, Beirut, Tyre, Sidon, Laodicea, Athens, Sparta, Cos, Rhodes, Samos, and many Ionian cities. Finally, he saved the Olympian games from decline, providing the people of Elis, who organized them, with special perpetual revenues for the purpose.

In Jerusalem itself he built an imposing fortress which he called the Antonia in honor of his friend and protector, the triumvir Mark Antony. It was there that the Roman procurators, Herod's successors, had their offices, their temporary quarters

70

Mea Shearim,
Orthodox Jewish quarter

for the periods when they climbed up to the holy city from Caesarea, together with offices and accommodation for the military garrison. A series of large-scale underground cisterns (which are still in existence) guaranteed prolonged resistance to any siege. In the center of the building there must have been a spacious courtyard (the Lithostratos) paved with huge slabs of stone, partly furrowed, some of which today are in a chapel of the Franciscan Convent of the Flagellation and the neighboring Ecce Homo Convent of the Sisters of Zion. It is possible that these stones may have been witnesses to the judgment of Pilate, the flagellation, and the crowning with thorns. The smoothest stones still bear the traces of markings used in the games of the Roman soliders, in their long days of service in this city on the edge of the world. One can also see the circle of the "king's game," used, during the Saturnalia, to elect the man who was going to preside over the festivities, enjoying all the honors but finally put to death.

At the other end of the city, to the southwest, Herod built the new royal palace: "Its buildings surpassed even the Temple in size and splendor," said Josephus. Nearby were the towers called Hippicus (after a friend), Phasael (in memory of a brother), and Mariamne (in memory of his wife). Parts of the base of one of the towers can still be seen today. The ashlar of big, roughly carved stones, giving the wall an appearance of craggy strength, is typical of the time of Herod. Evidently this building technique was brought to Europe by the Crusaders; it is possible that the Florentine palaces, with their air of fortress and private house combined, have some remote stylistic connection with Herod's Jerusalem.

Herod's palace remained standing until the time of Hadrian, then it fell into ruins. One of the towers was identified with older works and was called the "Tower of David," and here apparently, in the Byzantine period, a number of hermits entrenched themselves.

The work dearest to Herod's heart was the rebuilding of the Temple. It is difficult to say whether he gave so much thought to this work, and lavished such riches upon it, because he felt that he would receive glory from it in the future, or whether he did it to curry favor with the Jews of whom he was king, but a king who aroused controversy, supported and accepted only at times and only in part. Perhaps the two motives merged one with the other. The fact remains that the work was tackled with the most detailed preparation, and the most lavish of means. The building of the new Temple seems to have been carried on as the old one was pulled down. Since only priests were allowed to enter certain parts, a thousand or so priests had to learn the craft of masons, bricklayers, and carpenters; there were also eighteen thousand ordinary workmen. Work was begun in 19 B.C., after the plans had been approved by the elders of the city and the cult, and it went on intermittently well after Herod's death, until A.D. 64. This date brings us nearly to the Jewish War and the capture of Jerusalem by Titus, the time when the new Temple, completed with such trouble and expense, was to be totally destroyed.

The old esplanade, originally obtained by extending a threshing floor, was no

Main street,
Mea Shearim

longer big enough to house the new porticoes and building; the rock had to be quarried out on the Antonia side—that is, the north—and more space obtained with impressive bastions to the south. The barely squared blocks of stone of the Wailing Wall give one an idea of how construction problems were tackled. When the work was completed a trapezium had been obtained which measured (as it still does) 500 and 534 yards by 304 and 363. On this light and airy esplanade, the present-day Haram-ash-Sharif with the Dome of the Rock and the Mosque of al-Aqsa, stood the various buildings of the Temple.

For the ancient Jews, the Temple was exclusively the abode of God, a point of the earth where God came down for his meetings with the faithful. This conception of the place of worship is profoundly different from the one prevalent among Christians, most Moslems, Buddhists, and Jews from the Diaspora onward, for whom churches, mosques, temples, and synagogues also house the faithful. The real Temple was small, squat, inaccessible; the only people who entered it were the priests, and even they did so only on certain specific occasions, according to ancient ritual. A complex organism of buildings and spaces had grown up around the Sanctuary. From here, through the Gate of Nicanor, up a semicircular staircase, one went to a courtyard. Another door, the Corinthia, another wall and one arrived at the Court of the Gentiles. Entry from the Court of the Gentiles beyond the Corinthian door in the direction of the interior was permitted to Jews alone. There still exists an example of the relevant warnings in Greek: "Let no foreigner venture beyond this barrier and the enclosure surrounding the Sanctuary. Anyone caught in the attempt will have been the cause of his own death."

The Temple of Jerusalem, though smaller than many other historical buildings, from the Parthenon to the temple of Marduk of Babylon, to say nothing of the temples of Baalbec or Rome itself, made a great impression on contemporaries. The decorations must have been rich and intricate, though there were no images of human beings. "Master, see what manner of stones and what buildings are here!" (Mark 13:1), and Luke speaks of its being "adorned with goodly stones and gifts" (Luke 21:5). Apparently a golden vine, the symbol of Israel, topped one of the entrances. Herod, according to Flavius Josephus, had put a great golden eagle on the arch of the main entrance. But this offended the religious feelings of the Jews because, according to a law of Moses, no image of a human being or of an animal should figure in the Temple. During Herod's last illness a group of the ardent faithful tore the eagle down; furious, Herod had the young culprits burned alive, together with two old doctors of the law who had instigated the act; justice was done on others involved, in less cruel ways.

Another of Herod's last acts was the notorious massacre of the Innocents (Matt. 2:16). The chronology is slightly confused: at first sight it would seem that the event could not have taken place, Herod having died in 4 B.C. But the chronology regarding the life of Christ is also much debated; the date of his birth should be anticipated by a few years, probably up to 6 B.C. Chronologically, therefore, the event is possible after all. It is true that no document of the time, apart from the Gospels, tells us of this massacre, but Herod left behind him a name stained with so many cruelties that this one would be quite in keeping.

As his last resting place Herod had a fortress built, about five miles from Bethlehem, which still stands and is known as the Herodium. Indeed, it is difficult to take a photograph of Bethlehem with its churches, from north or west, without having the bulk of the Herodium in the background. This offers a marvelously edifying cue to anyone wanting to elaborate on the vanity of human affairs, particularly when one considers that thousands and thousands of people flood in from all parts of the world to the churches in the foreground, to honor the birthplace of one of Herod the Great's humblest subjects.

Shortly after Herod's death disturbances broke out in Judaea. Herod's son Archelaus was not popular. The Romans had to intervene, and there were savage operations, of the kind that today we call "pacification," in which at least two thousand rebels were crucified. The Romans were not slow to realize that it was impossible to govern through Archelaus, and they replaced him with an imperial procurator. Archelaus was relegated to Vienne in Gaul (a town now noted for one of the best restaurants in the world, but then a not very alluring provincial frontier post). The procurator governed Judaea, Samaria, and Idumaea; he was subordinate to the legate of Syria, who had legions at his disposal to keep the peace. The procurator had to live in Caesarea and could go to Jerusalem only for the great annual festivals. The Jews were left free to practice their religion as they wished. Respect was accorded to religious feelings, banners with effigies of emperors were forbidden in the city, and there was a special dispensation regarding acts of worship of deified emperors. The coinage did not bear images, either. Lastly, we know that every day Augustus had a bull and two rams sacrificed on the Temple altar, for his own health and that of the Roman people.

By and large it seemed as though the problems of turbulent Judaea had been resolved; the procurators succeeded one another with the regularity of officials of a solid colonial administration; the people tended to their own affairs, followed the dictates and rites of their religion, and celebrated its important festivals. From A.D. 6 to 71 there were seven procurators. One, active from 26 to 36, bore a name which certain events in Jerusalem's municipal history were to render famous: Pontius Pilate. Shortly afterward, for three years (41–44) there was another king, Herod Agrippa (grandson of Herod the Great), who managed to get his position through Caligula and who, as the historian Parkes tells us, "unexpectedly proved a good ruler." Of the remaining procurators some, like Valerius Gratus, were honest men, while others, like Gessius Florus, an adventurer who obtained the post through the intrigues of a high-ranking courtesan sister, were crooks.

In reality Jews and Romans found it hard to get on with one another. Gone were the days when Judas Maccabaeus sang the praises of Rome and its senate. It is true that those had been Romans of the Republic, that things had changed a good deal first with the Principate and then the Empire, but in practice the Romans had shown themselves to be like all other wielders of power. Finally, there was a basic lack of understanding between the two peoples, a gulf deeper than that dividing Jews and Greeks. A man educated with the Greek view of life would find many of the Jews' customs odd, their literature rough, the myth of Yahweh excessive, but there did exist at least a potential meeting ground in their common passion for matters of the mind. The day when a big branch of the Jewish trunk, Christianity, was transplanted onto Greek soil, it was immediately able to flourish and bear fruit. Early Christianity was an exquisite synthesis of Hebrew and Greek elements: the very words "presbyter," "ecclesia," "episcopacy," "eucharist," "Christ," and many others bear witness to this union. But these things meant little to the Romans. Guignebert has noted that the Romans, except those from North Africa, who were of course provincials, made very few contributions to the development of early Christianity, limiting themselves to the disciplinary and organizational aspects of religious life. The Romans never managed to understand the Jews, with all their scruples, phobias, quirks, and the Jews saw the Romans as illustrating the triumph of materialism and godlessness and hated them for their continual offenses against the purity of the faith.

When the new Roman commander in the East, Pompey, after days of fierce fighting and after his men had marched over the broken bodies of thousands of Jews, finally managed to penetrate the Holy of Holies—according to Tacitus—he was amazed to find an empty cell. All those months of resistance, all that blood, all the suffering, for what? To defend empty air! "Jerusalem was conquered; but it remained inexplicable," as Join-Lambert rightly observed. In any case one need only read the Apocalypse to sense the absolute, total, final, organic, physical disgust felt by the Jews for Rome, for all its empire stood for. Not being able to name it directly, John called it Babylon; in his capacity as wizard, *magicien ès visions,* he made it a whore who had fornicated with every king on earth, a hideous scarlet creature with seven heads (the hills); when he spoke of Rome the veins of his neck must have swelled, saliva must have spurted from his lips, he was as wild as a great Tibetan Buddha at his most ferocious, his member erect in front of his stomach, surrounded by haloes of flame, ready to exterminate the forces of evil.

During the decades of Rome's rule the pressure mounted relentlessly, like steam in a boiler without a safety valve.

74

XII | THE UNIVERSE, A SERIES OF EVENTS

In the Greek and Roman world the sense of history was not, generally speaking, very deep nor was history philosophically important. The myth of the four ages (gold, silver, bronze, and iron), possibly of Eastern origin, prevailed, or else a cyclical conception, the myth of the eternal return, with the same things repeated after a greater or lesser period of time, as Marcus Aurelius wrote in his notes. The systems of the philosophers naturally did contain a complete anthropology, but human destiny was seen in a universal setting; specific facts of history were not regarded as deeply significant.

According to Hebrew thought, history was an absolutely essential element in the conception of the world. The universe was not so much a place as a series of events. The creation of men and their successive relations with God, outlined in precise, historical circumstances, made up the great cosmic drama, the only one that had any sense or value. Between God and man there were pacts, then breaches and subsequent punishments; but God was magnanimous, there were more pacts—and then man failed again. The observance of these pacts brought success and victory, breaking them meant exposure to often disastrous grief and humiliation. These were not abstract textbook cycles: they were concrete cycles, with geographical and chronological limits, real history, or so it was believed, which came to the same thing.

God created the first couple; he made an agreement with them; they did not keep their part of the bargain, and their first troubles ensued. Men went from bad to worse, and there was a serious crisis, the Flood. Only one just man, Noah, was saved, with his family. This was the first example of the concept of the "remnant." The Lord was a terrible enemy; when he struck he scattered death mercilessly, yet he did not abandon men completely, there was always a nucleus of survivors (the "remnant"), enabling humanity to continue. Thus history proceeded with its new pacts, with Abraham, with Moses, until the glory of the reigns of David and Solomon.

The oldest Biblical texts—written shortly after the period of the kings, according to experts—particularly the so-called Yahwistic ones, express a bloody and barbaric sense of certainty on the part of the people, and celebrate a masterly rule exerted by Yahweh, powerful and generous. The promises had been kept. Israel had occupied Canaan, the people had lands, a king, peace; "Judah and Israel dwelt in safety, every man under his vine and under his fig tree, from Dan even to Beersheba" (I Kings 4:25).

In the texts of slightly more recent times (seventh to sixth centuries B.C.), when

75

the rulers after Solomon were going from bad to worse and the threat, first of the Assyrians and then of the Babylonians, emerged ever more clearly, the theme of fall and punishment became predominant. Man was more uncertain, more doubtful, weaker. The prophets of the time (Amos, Isaiah, Jeremiah) deliver mainly threats, anathemas, heartfelt invitations to repent; they present visions of trouble, ruin, disaster, and despair. The theme of grief reaches sublimity (and the peak of despair) in Jeremiah, who was living during the tragic events of the fall of Jerusalem (587) and saw his people taken off into exile.

After this period of terrible trial, with the return to Jerusalem, a new era began. God's punishment had been cruel, but in a sense it was redemptive; the very fact that he allowed the return was a sign of forgiveness. We are "the remnant"—the survivors seemed to say—now a new page of the world's history is beginning. The texts which, according to the experts, bear the most genuine mark of this period, those by the priestly author, or authors, reflect the new spirit. Let us be guided by the past; the Lord can save or damn; in his revelations he has shown us the right way, let us therefore try to keep to it if we want a future of peace and prosperity: hence scrupulous attention to the rites and duties of the faithful and the citizen; ritual cherished as a form of redemption.

This was the time when the Pentateuch (Torah) took on what was probably its final shape. The word "law," with which it is often denominated, does not translate from one language to another the wealth of meanings of the word. "Torah" is one of those key words of a civilization—like "truth," "beauty," "justice" in the West; "dharma," "karma," "nirvana," in India and the other lands of Buddhism; "Tien," "Tao," "li" in China; "kami," "makoto," "kokoro" in Japan—which act as pillars to a whole vision of the world and of life. The Torah is also a theology and a cosmology, but above all it is a "complete plan, for society and the nation, to guide everyday life. Its precepts concern every aspect of life, domestic, social, commercial, legal, and even political," as James Parkes observes in his *History of the Jewish People*. Furthermore, with the passing of time, ever broader meanings accrued to the Torah, which came to include the whole body of Hebrew knowledge and tradition, therefore everything contained in the other books of the Bible, the Talmud, and the canonic literature of the Jewish people.

If the return from Babylon to Jerusalem marked a rebirth of the Jewish people, their subordinate position first under the Persians and then under the Ptolemies ended by discouraging those who had dreamed of a future return to real freedom, to the splendors of the old kingdom. Also, when the Syrian Greeks took the place of the Egyptians, the people's sufferings and humiliation knew no bounds. At this point they began to feel a creeping lack of confidence in the present world, of life as it was. If not even strict observance of the law, practiced from Ezra onward, could lead to peace and freedom, to a state of normal well-being, what was left?

At the same time, in contrast, a general interest emerged in the words of those forecasting, at least for the distant future, vistas of liberation, revenge, radical change

76

in the condition of the Hebrew people. The old concept of the Messiah acquired new warmth and urgency, new richness and diversity: some saw him as a descendant of the house of David who would appear, sword in hand, to drive away the foreigners and restore its supreme glory to the throne of Jerusalem; others, conversely, saw him as a humble liberator, a harbinger of peace.

This flight from reality, this consolation in hopes and myth, took luxuriant shape in another field, too, that of apocalyptic literature. The prophet Ezekiel was one of the first to point the way; others, famous like Daniel or obscure like the authors of many apocryphal texts, followed him with ever greater success. The word "Apocalypse," literally "revelation," later came to mean texts which told of fantastic visions about heaven, God, angels, cosmic upheavals which were to accompany the "day of the Lord," the arrival of the Messiah, and the establishment of a new order in the world.

This period also saw the development of certain movements of thought, some of which soon acquired political significance too. From the time of the Maccabees onward two important currents had emerged, that of the Pharisees (the word means "separated," probably from the religiously lax ones) and that of the Sadducees (who took their name from the family of the High Priest of King David, Zadok). What distinguished them was a different attitude to the Torah. The Pharisees accepted an oral tradition parallel to the written one and admitted the interpretation of the law, provided it was formulated and promulgated by an expert in the field; the Sadducees kept strictly to the letter of the written text. The Pharisees were ready to admit certain modifications and evolutions of faith. The Sadducees were rigorously conservative. The Pharisees were more fanatical and radical, partly because they had spent a long period of time in opposition while the Sadducees, holding the high posts in the Temple, were for the established order. The Pharisees had more support among the people, while the Sadducees were always ready to reach agreement with foreigners. It was the eternal dilemma between right and left.

All this runs counter to the traditional picture of the Pharisees but it is now recognized that they are shown at their worst in the Gospels, for polemical reasons. Admitting interpretation of the law, the Pharisees tended to discuss endlessly points of doctrine and procedure. But their philosophical and exegetic vitality was creative; it led to dynamic activity, in contrast with the conservatism of the Sadducees. The Pharisees, for instance, accepted a doctrine of individual immortality that was denied by the Sadducees, who remained faithful to the old conception of *Sheol*, a kingdom of shades. Finally, one should remember that in A.D. 70, when the Temple was destroyed, the Sadducees disappeared from the face of the earth, leaving the Pharisees as heirs of virtually the whole Jewish tradition. It is from them that Talmudic Judaism, the Judaism of the Diaspora, descends, the Judaism that is with us today (apart from the small sect of Karaites, who, like the Sadducees of old, recognize only the Bible and the Talmud).

Besides these two main currents there were also others of varying importance,

77

arising from different interpretations of messianic ideas then generally current and accepted. Asserting that the present order was completely corrupt, irredeemable, unbearable, that salvation could come only from the establishment of an entirely new order by the work of some supernatural agent, people given to extreme solutions had a choice of attitude. On the one hand, they could try to hasten the advent of the *novus ordo* by rebellion, joining partisan guerrilla fighters—which was the case of the Zealots and numerous other groups about which we have only vague information because the leaders fell into the hands of procurators and were brought to justice. On the other hand, it was logical completely to reject the world, to withdraw from it and await "the day of the Lord," leading a holy, ascetic, monastic life of spiritual preparation. This was the way chosen, for instance, by the Essenes.

Flavius Josephus tells about these Essenes at length; they lived in communities mostly, though not exclusively, of single men; they pooled their personal belongings, rejected war, slavery, trade; they tried to keep themselves in a state of complete independence, tilling the fields; they also aimed at a life of study and meditation in absolute purity. In many ways, the Essenes were the true precursors of medieval monasticism.

Since 1947 the Essenes have been much discussed in connection with a community situated at Qumran, on the Dead Sea. It is by no means certain that this community was one of Essenes; but it is certain that its members rejected the world, as it then was, in order to await the Messiah, or Master of Justice, the very Master who had initiated their movement. In the caves inhabited by this community were found precious documents (the Dead Sea Scrolls) which are providing us with religious texts of the greatest importance. The copies of the known texts are about one thousand years older than those available hitherto; there have also appeared works, or fragments of works, up to now completely unknown.

Looking generally at the Judaea of the first century A.D., one has therefore to reconsider many traditionally accepted ideas. This period is known mainly through what we are told in the New Testament and by the historian Flavius Josephus. Now, both the authors of the New Testament and Josephus, for reasons it would take too long to analyze here, are strongly pro-Roman. In their pages the centurions, soldiers, even the hated publicans who collected the taxes, are presented in a particularly favorable light, as just men stricken by the miserable fate of being born at the wrong time. Pontius Pilate, whom other impartial sources reveal as cruel and tyrannical (he was recalled to Rome for an unjustified massacre of Samaritans), was saved by the washing of his hands and one magnanimous sentence. As for Flavius Josephus, when he talks of bandits it is clear that he is referring to what we today would call "partisans" in the guerrilla fighting against Rome. Documents revealing the point of view of the oppressed in Judaea are rare—yet the New Testament Apocalypse speaks quite clearly. We can only guess, from sporadic episodes or a few marginal observations, how heavily the Roman yoke fell on every aspect of life.

This external pressure fed unceasing and widespread messianic hopes, which

78

were strengthened by the words of the ancient prophets. Some saw the Messiah as a heavenly warrior-sovereign, others as a master, a holy man. The very variety of these ideal projections revealed the vitality of the tendencies and movements of the period. The traditional image of a Pharisaic sleep, suddenly shattered by an exceptional event, needs to be completely revised. Apart from what was going on in the minds of the Essenes, the Pharisees of various schools, the Sadducees, Zealots, hermits of Qumran, Nazarenes, and yet other groups in the line of the Judaic tradition, one should also take into account the echoes, far from feeble, of the thought and myths of the Hellenistic and Oriental worlds. Neo-Pythagoreanism, Platonism, Gnosticism, the solar cults, the Persian religion, even India, left traces in the documents of those times, which were times of torment and anguish but also of a liveliness that makes them particularly close to us.

This political and social, cultural and religious scene formed the setting, in the second decade of our era, for the preaching of a young carpenter from Galilee, Yeshua bar Yoseph, better known by his Latinized name of Jesus. His teaching turned on two essential points: first, the kingdom of God (or heaven) is at hand; secondly, let us prepare ourselves for its advent with a pure heart.

Who was Jesus? What did he really teach? Was he a Jewish reformer, like so many others, or the founder of a new religion? Was he a meek man or a rebel? Until the end of the last century, he was seen almost universally in the light of apotheosis cast upon him by the disciples and Paul of Tarsus. He was the son of God, the Word made Flesh, the Messiah descended among men to redeem them by a glorious death on the cross, and a miraculous resurrection three days later, from the original sin of the couple who fathered all mankind.

For a century and a half historians, using all available means, old and new, from textual analysis to carbon 14, from archaeology to numismatics, have tried to throw light on the man who gave birth to the greatest spiritual movement recorded by history and on the earliest days of the church born of his ministry. Documents are so scarce that a whole school—Kalthoff, Smith, Drews, and others—have been seen to try to find a positively paradoxical solution: to explain Christianity without Christ. "He never existed, He is a solar myth, a new impersonation of the Sumerian and Babylonian hero Gilgamesh." It has even been said: "Christianity is conceivable without Jesus, not without Paul of Tarsus." Then there are the famous interpretations by the authors who have tried to make a real man out of him, the subject of minute chronicle and biography; this is the Jesus of Renan, Papini, Pier Paolo Pasolini. Since the discovery of the Dead Sea Scrolls, some have tried to identify him with the Master of Justice, or at least to link him closely with the cenobites of Qumran. Another recent school sees in Jesus a charismatic and unfortunate leader in the desperate struggles of the Jews against Rome.

These and other considerations, which historians will be able to elaborate in greater depth, may perhaps bear weight in the future. To interpolate a completely personal view, I feel that man is moving toward a plane where truths established by

Mea Shearim

free research will have an ever greater weight, such as finally to shatter the shell of any myth, any revelation whatever. If historical research could show, to the general satisfaction, that, let us say, Jesus had been an unlucky guerrilla idealist, a rebel against the foreign tyranny of his time, that he tried to spread a more intimate and spontaneous interpretation of the Jewish religion than the formalist one then current, and that, as a result of this, through a cumulation of historically ascertainable facts, his life, teaching, and death became an integral part of the cosmic conceptions of a world where messianic expectation was widespread, to the point of complete apotheosis in the identification of the man with the Man, Man with the Word, and the Word with God, this truth or any other resulting from it would be infinitely more religious than the traditional one. Religious in the sense that it would adhere more strictly to the secret and august mechanisms of history, to the genuine movements of the human soul in its age-old creative efforts to cast bridges toward the unknown.

Shop on Jaffa Street

XIII | A CITY DESTROYED

In the setting of the Mediterranean world of the time, Jesus' death on the cross was not an event of resounding consequence. Anyone living in Jerusalem at that time would often have heard of men being crucified, decapitated, or dealt with in more or less cruel ways. Of one it might be said: "He was a hero," of another: "He was a holy man," or alternatively: "But they were only outlaws and impostors!" The time of a heavy, hated occupation is a gloomy one. All that has come down to us from those distant years are mere names—Judas of Galilee, a founder of the fourth philosophic sect among the Jews and a leader of last-ditch resistance to any religious imposition; Theudas, a pseudo-messianic magician, and James and Simon, Judas's sons, both crucified—but there is no knowing how many perished in unspeakable agony to keep faith with misunderstood and derided principles, or simply for freedom, or for both. The disciples of Jesus, who for them was now the Lord's Anointed, the Messiah, Christ, at first formed an obscure Jewish sect to be added to those already existing at that time and in that place.

There was a brief interlude of calm during the reign (40–44) of Herod Agrippa, grandson of Herod the Great, whose memory left favorable echoes even in the Talmud (Mishnah Bikk. III: 4, Mishnah Sota VII: 8, and elsewhere). The procurators who succeeded him brought tension back to the breaking point. Acts of rebellion, sporadic at first, became so frequent that Judaea was soon prey to bands of guerrillas and on the threshold of real war. "Rebels of another sort, known as sicarii, appeared in Jerusalem. They performed their assassinations in broad daylight, in the very heart of the city," said Flavius Josephus. This would be the equivalent of plastic bombs, or snipers shooting from rooftops.

The uneasy peace was definitively broken when the procurator Gessius Florus ordered the massacre of a deputation that was attempting to present requests to him in an orderly way. This time no means could placate the people's fury. A small group of rebels seized the Temple and barricaded themselves within it. In vain King Agrippa II of Chalcis, who was passing through the city, delivered a long speech— reported at length in Josephus—trying to calm their wrath and demonstrating the power of Rome with consummate oratory; he was seized and stoned. By now it was too late for an understanding. Another group of rebels, led by Menahem, son of Judas of Galilee, had set off meanwhile for Masada on the Dead Sea. Masada is the name of a flat-topped hill *(bambah)* or high plateau entirely surrounded by almost perpendicular cliffs; Herod the Great had had it fortified so that it was an almost impregnable bastion. The Roman garrison occupying it, surprised in their sleep, were overwhelmed and the rebels took their places. The Jerusalem group, under Eleazar, reinforced by more rebels, managed not only to hold the Temple but to drive the Romans from the Antonia, so that they had to take refuge in Herod's palace, near what today is the Jaffa Gate.

Shortly afterward, Menahem and some of the group who had occupied Masada arrived in Jerusalem; they were seized and killed. As a revenge the Jews slew all the Roman soldiers they could lay hands on. Then the Romans of Caesarea, soldiers and civilians, massacred the Jews in that city. The war of liberation had begun; all Judaea became a prey to violence.

At this point all that could be done was to ask for help from the Syrian legate, who had reliable troops available. A force of thirty thousand men went into Palestine and managed to pacify Galilee—incidentally, taking prisoner Flavius Josephus, who was later to write the famous history of the war, as well as other works intended to glorify the civilization and religion of the Jews for the readers of the Greco-Roman world. The rebels who did not intend to surrender joined the others who were still masters of Jerusalem.

Rome, seeing that operations in Judaea were lagging, sent a trusted general, Vespasian, who pacified much of the territory; then Nero's suicide created sudden problems of succession, and there was a brief period of uncertainty (the "year of the four emperors," A.D. 68–69). Finally Vespasian emerged triumphant. Operations in Judaea were entrusted to his son Titus, who wanted to plan his attack on Jerusalem in meticulous detail. Titus gathered an army of sixty-five thousand men, and on May 10, A.D. 70, he arrived beneath the walls of the city. The rebels were not all of one mind, nor did they have the same plans. There were extremists (led by John of Gischala) and moderates; the clashes between the two groups had wreaked havoc in the countryside and ruined the harvest; the siege promised great hardship because of the scarcity of supplies available.

It is interesting to note that Josephus—when he was about to be taken prisoner, after the fall of Jotapata—addressed a prayer to God in which he said: "Since it pleaseth thee, who hath created the Jewish nation, now to level it with the dust and transfer its fortune to the Romans..." With these words Josephus, who in his works almost always reveals himself as thoroughly Hellenized, who speaks of Fate and Virtue, here shows himself inspired by a concept most typical of Jewish thought. The Romans' good luck was seen as a choice of the God of Israel; the Romans were hailed as the new chosen people. It was quite logical therefore for Josephus to transfer his own loyalty to them—staining himself for all eternity with the charge of traitor in the eyes of his compatriots and fellow Jews.

The most determined rebels, those who intended to carry on the struggle to the death, commanded by John of Gischala, took refuge in the stronghold of the rebellion, Jerusalem. The siege operations continued uninterruptedly from May to September. Josephus, who followed the Roman forces as a sort of "expert in Jewish affairs," tells us of the phases of the siege with the immediacy of a war correspondent.

82

There were 23,400 armed defenders in the city, divided into two groups, one under the command of Simon bar-Giora, the other under John of Gischala. For some time the two factions kept up their rivalries; it was only after the first determined assaults by the Romans that they decided to join forces. Apart from these military units, the city must also have been harboring many thousands of ordinary citizens within its walls.

After two weeks the Romans managed to get inside the first circle of the walls; a few days later they were through to the second, but the Antonia fortress, the Temple, and the high part of the city resisted valiantly. Hunger was rampant, turning men into beasts. Anyone suspected of hiding food was tortured until he revealed his secret. Anyone who tried to creep out of the city might be taken by the Romans and crucified in front of the walls to frighten the rebels. The extremists had long since passed the point when they could withdraw or surrender. *Certa morte ferociores,* further incited by their leaders, who were shouting "God will save us," they fought desperately against the Romans and savagely repressed any signs of yielding on the part of the citizens. Such was the hunger that "a profound silence and a sort of mortal night" fell upon the city.

To make their engines of war, the Romans had felled all the trees within a radius of twelve miles of the city. Finally, one night, the Antonia was taken. It was August. No sooner had the Romans broken into it than an indescribable melee followed: "Because the place of battle was so narrow," says Josephus, "the adversaries were so intermingled that it was impossible to distinguish which side the respective combatants were on. There was no room for flight or pursuit. Confused reversals and turns succeeded one another. Necessity compelled the front-rank men to kill or be killed."

But the end had not yet come. The Romans had to retire and make further preparations. They razed the Antonia to the ground. In a sortie, the Jews attacked the Roman encampment on the Mount of Olives. The Romans came back to the Temple with new machines. Someone threw in a lighted torch, and the fire caught. Now there was no escape. Titus, it seems, had wanted to spare the Temple, but madness was abroad; the Jews preferred to see their shrine destroyed rather than yield it intact, and the Romans wanted to get their revenge for the spectacular resistance they had met with.

Once again desperadoes barricaded themselves in the uppermost part of the city, in the towers that made Herod's palace almost a second fortress, and resisted there for several days. A curious detail of those terrible moments: secretly, a man named Jesus offered Titus one of the Temple's candelabra, possibly the one we see carved on the arch of Titus in Rome. Only in September, after 139 days of struggle, was the city completely subdued. Oddly enough, the day the Temple fell coincided with that on which the first Temple had fallen to Nebuchadnezzar 657 years earlier. Two towers of Herod's palace were left standing, "as demonstration to posterity of how splendid and powerful a city had yielded to Roman valor" (Josephus). Tens of

Courtyard,
Bezalel quarter

thousands of prisoners were taken, sold as slaves, or thrown into circuses to be killed as gladiators; the seven hundred youngest and most handsome were taken to Rome, with Simon bar-Giora, to accompany Titus in the triumphal procession. While the procession passed in front of the temple of Jupiter Capitolinus, a shout of joy went up from crowd and soldiers: the leader of the enemy, Simon, had been killed on the open space above the Forum, where condemned evildoers were put to death. Then Vespasian and Titus initiated the sacrifices in honor of the gods.

In Judaea, however, there was still a certain amount of resistance. Three important fortresses had been left standing: the Herodium, Machaerus, and Masada. The first two fell without much struggle; but Masada was a special undertaking. A thousand or so sicarii under Eleazar had taken refuge there with ample stores of food, while water was supplied by huge cisterns. The plateaulike hill of Masada was defended all around by virtually unscalable precipices, but the Romans managed to pile up so much earth on the side where the precipice was lowest that at last a war machine was able to reach the walls with a battering ram and break them down. Now the way to the fortress was open. The Romans withdrew to make the final assault the following day.

During the night, or very early the next morning, Eleazar gathered his men and addressed them with fiery words. Josephus reports them in full. Through the ambiguous golden cloud of classical rhetoric we glimpse their terrible purport with emotion. Here is a passage: "It is very plain that we shall be taken within a day's time, but it is still an eligible thing to die after a glorious manner, together with our dearest friends.... Let our wives die before they are abused, and our children before they have tasted of slavery; and after we have slain them, let us bestow that glorious benefit upon one another mutually...."

After a brief moment of uncertainty everyone was in agreement. The men killed their own wives and children and then, holding the dead bodies of their loved ones, offered their own throats to the last ten, chosen by lot, to slaughter them. These ten, drawing further lots, killed one another. By now all was in flames. Masada was peopled only by the dead. The Romans entered later, amazed by "such fearful desolation" and possibly suspecting a trap. They called out, to give themselves courage. No one answered. At last, from a hiding place in the aqueduct, two women and some children emerged, the only ones who had managed to escape the madness of Eleazar and his men. Then the Romans learned what had happened; they went forward and saw the piles of dead: 960 in all, including women and children. "They did not exult over them as enemies, but admired the nobility of their resolve," Josephus commented.

Now new coins were in circulation in Judaea; on one face there was a palm tree with a Roman legionary to the left, with his staff of command and one foot on a helmet; to the right sat a weeping woman. The inscription read: *"Judaea devicta Judaea capta."* And indeed Judaea had good reason to weep: hundreds of thousands of Jews were sold as slaves in all the Mediterranean countries. This time the Diaspora

84

was one of the worst. Each national disaster—and there had been many since Nebuchadnezzar's destruction of Jerusalem—had led many groups of Jews to migrate. The idea that there was only one Diaspora, in about A.D. 70, is a gross historical simplification. Jewish communities had existed for centuries in Alexandria, Babylon, Cyrene, in the Greek world, in Syria; the new disaster created new centers, but above all it strengthened those already in existence. The Jews were inconvenient as slaves because of the ritual commitments that punctuated their day, their special food, and so on. But they worked well, and they soon earned their freedom. Once freed, they rarely allowed themselves to be assimilated by the surrounding societies; they constituted an isolated community which tended to live with its own laws and habits.

This new exile, as had happened in other cases of national disaster, led the Jews to fall back upon themselves, to work over their own spiritual heritage once again. The result was the final canon of the holy texts of the Bible: now that all other ties were broken, now that exile was the normal condition for most Jews, their God's word became the supreme link, the sign of a national identity. Now the Jews truly could be called the "People of the Book."

In about 130 Hadrian, in one of his endless journeys through his empire, passed through Syria and decided to rebuild Jerusalem, which was still in ruins, not as the city of David or Nehemiah, or even of Herod, but on a new plan, entirely in accordance with the rules and spirit of Greco-Roman town planning. Even a new name, Aelia Capitolina, was to replace the age-old one of Jerusalem. Hadrian, always a great admirer of the Greeks, could not understand the Jews, their inexplicable "superstitions" seemed absurd to him, and he thought of the most fanatical exponents of Judaism as "real enemies of the human race" who should be brought to the right path of civilized living with reason but also possibly with force. An airy Greco-Roman city on Mount Zion, with straight roads, colonnades, a capitol, forums, temples, amphitheaters, baths, and basilicas would be not only a sign of conquest but also a beacon of civilization. This topographical clean sweep would be accompanied by a parallel revolution in customs and affairs of the spirit. Circumcision, for instance—how barbaric! The human body must be respected.

Once again the Jews felt that their most sacred principles had been attacked—observance of the law, their memories of their shattered country. The deportations had been sweeping, but there were still many of the faithful in the various cities of Palestine; the boldest of them gathered around a last leader, Simon bar Kochba, proclaimed as Messiah by the famous rabbi, Akiba. For some time luck was with Simon, partly because he kept rebellion firmly in hand and used guerrilla tactics. But the Romans did not intend to yield: Jerusalem, which the rebels had occupied, was retaken in 133. Simon himself, with the last of the faithful, was hunted down and killed two years later.

85

Thabor house,
Street of the Prophets

This was the end, for Jerusalem. Until then the Romans had shown some respect for the feelings of the conquered; from 135 onward they were pitiless. The Jews were forbidden even to put foot in Aelia Capitolina; and on one of the triumphal arches that were the gates of the city was carved the emblem of the Tenth Legion, that impure animal, the wild boar.

What little remained of the Temple was destroyed. All that was left on the esplanade was the mysterious rock of Abraham, which no strength of the time would have been sufficient to remove. In place of the Temple, statues were put up to pagan divinities, monuments to Antony and Hadrian. Aelia was rebuilt. The Roman architects traced a great Cardo from north to south, a Decuman from east to west, lines that can still be followed today in the topography of the Old City. A forum grew up—about where the Holy Sepulcher is today—and temples were built in honor of Jupiter Capitolinus, Juno, and Venus Aphrodite. In a city that was to symbolize the unity of civilization, binding together all the lands of the West, from Britain to Syria, from Egypt to Noricum, there had to be a theater, circus, baths, the public buildings which distinguished the Roman world from that of the barbarians. The walls were not rebuilt; unlike Jerusalem, Aelia was not to be a fortified town. Apparently there were gates—or rather triumphal arches—marking the entrance to the city proper. Portions of these gates still survive in the arch of Ecce Homo, near the Convent of the Sisters of Zion.

Right
Monastery of the Cross, detail

Next two pages
Monastery of the Cross

XIV | ANASTASIS, RESURRECTION

This was pagan Jerusalem. It lasted a little less than two centuries, but supplanted almost completely the Jerusalem of the time of Jesus, of which there were only very few and doubtful remains. "Christian Jerusalem," Join-Lambert rightly remarks, "was not the successor to the Jewish city. She was a converted pagan city."

The disaster of the year 70 had a decisive influence on the development of an obscure Jewish sect, which had emerged a few decades earlier, whose followers were known as Messianists but were, in fact, "Christians." The small church of Jerusalem, led for some years by the apostle James, "our Lord's brother," had long been at loggerheads with its sister church at Antioch, where Paul of Tarsus had risen to preach, claiming a personal and direct revelation from Christ himself. Essentially the disagreement hinged on this question: Should the newly converted Gentiles obey the Mosaic law? Should they be circumcised, abstain from the forbidden foods, follow the other 613 commandments of the Torah? Jerusalem said Yes; Antioch, No. The matter might seem relatively unimportant, but its solution one way or the other was to have a decisive effect on the whole future of Christ's teaching. In the one case the "Christians" would continue to belong to a small dissident Jewish sect, one of the many throughout the centuries; in the other a new religion was about to be born, the daughter of Judaism but alive, precisely, with all the independence that children have of their parents. The dispute was still raging when the rebellion of 66 broke out, then the war and confusion of 70, the final suspension of sacrifices in the Temple, the fall of Jerusalem. The fathers of the local church fled to Pella, where, known as the Ebionites, they apparently kept the congregation alive for some time. Events had decided in favor of Antioch: the cult of the risen Messiah was to be the nucleus of a new religion, the faithful would no longer be bound by Mosaic law, a new "covenant" between God and men was replacing the old one. A new universal religion had emerged; the faithful constituted the new Israel, no longer of the flesh, but of the spirit.

The Jews were forbidden to set foot in Jerusalem, but not the Gentiles who happened to be Christians. From the second century A.D. a small nucleus of the faithful apparently settled in the city of the Passion, and perhaps the very first church arose on Mount Zion, where the so-called Chapel of the Last Supper is still standing. Too many memories were linked with Jerusalem for it to be forgotten; the idea of journeying to the Holy Land to visit the places of the Passion and Resurrection soon became very popular: Alexander Flavian and Origen were among the first illustrious pilgrims to the holy places. But this beginning of local Christian life was soon inter-

87

Monastery of the Cross, entrance

rupted by the persecutions, begun by Decius in 250 and becoming really ferocious under Diocletian and Maximinus at the beginning of the fourth century.

Yet the new faith, however persecuted, or perhaps because it was persecuted, triumphed. With the Edict of Milan (313) the Christians were granted freedom of worship. Within a few years Jerusalem underwent another of its innumerable transformations and became a splendid Christian holy city, rich with sumptuous shrines, basilicas, monasteries, churches recording the various episodes in Christ's earthly life and that of the saints. Once upon a time the Jewish temples had been destroyed to make way for those of pagan cults; now—as Eusebius of Caesarea says—these same buildings, "which had been erected by fraud, were thrown to the ground from their full height and the seats of the false gods were deprived and purged of their statues." The impassive and infinitely ancient stones of the golden city must have wondered what new whirlwind had burst in upon the heart of man, never weary of rebuilding. As for the Jews, the Christian masters of the city were happy to inherit the ban put upon them by the pagans. With subtle arguments, the Fathers of the Church established that the Jews, having refused to recognize Christ as the true Messiah, had lost all right to the city and the Temple. Let them stay outside it, then, as they had done for so many generations.

For a short time the Emperor Julian (331–363) attempted to restore the religion of his fathers, opposing what seemed to him a ruinous departure from the very roots of Greek and Roman civilization. In 362 he allowed the Jews to go back to Jerusalem, where they made initial preparations to rebuild the Temple. But Julian died the following year, and the Jews had to leave the city once again. Many laws and rites of the old religion had been forgotten or transcended by the new one born of it; but one, unfortunately, had passed from mother to daughter—intolerance. "It is just," Emperor Justinian was later to write, "to deprive of their earthly goods those who do not worship the true God."

From the first decades of the fourth century Bishop Macarius, fully authorized by Emperor Constantine, had begun to search under the new buildings of Aelia Capitolina for the traces, and ultimately relics, of Jesus' passage through the city. His tomb was found, apparently, beneath the temple of Venus—which was promptly demolished—and plans were made for an impressive series of shrines. Even the Emperor's mother, Helena, recently converted to Christianity, went to Jerusalem with all the ardor of an elderly noblewoman seeking pardon for the sins of a stormy youth. In no time she had founded a basilica on the Mount of Olives and another at Bethlehem. According to information dating from a few decades after the fact, the Empress also discovered, not only the rocky height on which Jesus' cross had been erected, but also, in a cistern not far away, the three crosses of Christ and the two criminals. A miracle (the curing of a sick man or the resurrection of a dead one, it is uncertain which) made it possible to identify the true cross. "The Finding of the Cross" became a favorite theme of Christian art, and centuries later Piero della Francesca painted one of the most magnificently inspired examples of it in Arezzo.

88

Together with the cross, the Empress also found the nails. It seems that one of them was thrown by her into the sea, to calm it, during a storm encountered when she was sailing back toward Byzantium; another ended up mysteriously in the iron crown of the Lombard kings. With the finding of the cross, and many other objects recalling Christ's Passion, the search for, the collection and veneration of relics, began. No one would wish to exclude the possibility that the very first ones were genuine, but with the passing of time, as pilgrims became increasingly numerous and relics ever more rare, a secret industry of objects passing as holy must have grown up to fool credulous and pious travelers. Only thus can one explain the fact that there are more than twenty "genuine" nails, dozens of foreskins in various shrines, supposedly belonging to the infant Jesus, and that the Virgin's milk can be measured in gallons. This mingling of sacred and profane, of candor and cunning, was quite human and natural in a city that was basically poor, where life was not entirely spent reciting tridua and novenas, antiphons and doxologies, but—as contemporary sources show—was also colored by clowns in taverns, whores and soothsayers, all kinds of curious riffraff who had come to Jerusalem to scrape a living from the pilgrims of all nations, languages, colors, and customs.

The buildings that Emperor Constantine had designed and built in Jerusalem, to mark the places where Jesus had spent his last worldly hours in torment and his first heavenly hours of resurrection in glory, were grandiose, simple, and noble in their basic conception. The actual tomb was covered with a great domed rotunda known as the Anastasis (Resurrection). Beyond the Anastasis, alongside the Cardo Maximus, there was an impressive basilica with five naves and an apse: the Martyrion. Between the Anastasis and the Martyrion was a circular atrium surrounded with columns; a similar atrium stood before the main entrance of the Martyrion, alongside the Cardo. The buildings thus made up a harmonious and organic whole, logically linked with the street and connecting the three main holy places—the tomb of Christ, Golgotha, and the well of the cross—so that they could be visited with ease along an itinerary evolving naturally and intuitively. There was also a Baptistery joined to the Anastasis.

The new buildings were dedicated on September 13, 335, with great pomp and solemnity. One may perhaps gain some idea of what they looked like by thinking of the oldest Roman basilicas. Unfortunately, the sanctuary was destroyed during successive episodes of violence. Today one can see the shape of the original Anastasis in its successor, and there are a few stretches of wall that may date back to Constantine—but that is all.

With all these huge and, one imagines, reading the descriptions that remain of them, remarkably beautiful buildings, Jerusalem was once more a religious center of prime importance, attracting visitors and pilgrims not only for its memories, but for its splendor: was it not "the hill which God desireth to dwell in" (Ps. 68:16)?

Apart from the main buildings, others were going up in the city and on the surrounding hills and valleys. On the Mount of Olives stood the basilica Eleona, and the Imbomon, an octagonal shrine topped by a dome, commemorating the Ascension on the spot where it was traditionally supposed to have taken place (Acts 1:12). To fortify the doubtful, from the earliest times what we today would call a legendary footprint of Jesus could be seen there. The earliest building dated from 362 and was founded, like so many others of the time, by a pious great lady. History also records her name—Pomenia—and she must have been very wealthy because the building was crowned by a gleaming cross (of gold?) visible from a great distance.

This invasion of Christian Jerusalem by women, and mainly wealthy ones, is worthy of note. We know the names of several of them: Helena, Constantine's mother, Melania, founder of a monastery and refuge for pilgrims on the Mount of Olives, her granddaughter, another Melania, then Pomenia, later Empress Eudocia, widow of Theodosius II, and others. One has a clear picture of these great ladies, holy and tireless, eager to instill order into the world, followed by reverend clerics with bows and smiles.

How different from the Jerusalem of the Temple! The Jews, too, had had prophetesses—Deborah, Huldah—and queens—Athaliah, Alexandra—but they had been exceptions. Everything concerned with the Temple and its cults was the province of men exclusively. The Jewish religion has kept its character of masculinity up to the present day. Perhaps that is why it is far from incompatible with war. It could be that the pious and well-meaning matrons of Jerusalem—like so many followers of Apollonius of Tyana in Rome in the remote past, Tagore in India not so long ago, and Krishnamurti in Switzerland or America today—might ultimately have saved the city from its destiny of fire and blood. But Jerusalem's years under the Christians were an interregnum. With the arrival of the Moslems in 636 there was a return to the Semitic regime, to a God who looked kindly upon women only if they stayed quietly at home.

There are still remains of the Imbomon on the Mount of Olives: particularly interesting is the edicule, apparently reminiscent of the original building of the Anastasis. The dome of the Imbomon, with its center open to the sky, had the same diameter as that of the Anastasis (11 meters); but it has long since disappeared. The building was completely restored, indeed practically rebuilt, by the Crusaders, and the small chapel, with its pointed arches and intertwined columns, is one of the jewels of medieval art plainly Frankish in influence. Moslem architects, successors to the Crusaders, rebuilt the dome in about 1200, and the result was heavy and disproportionate.

What remains of these various architectual superimpositions constitutes one of the typical Jerusalem clusters in which places, memories, languages, traditions, and cultures intertwine to produce syntheses of spontaneous and total ecumenism.

Part of the building serves as the residence of a Moslem imam; beneath it is an ancient tomb which the Jews traditionally regard as that of the prophetess Huldah, while Christians connect it with the name and adventures of a certain Pelagia, a beautiful actress from Antioch who became converted to a life of asceticism and

90

lived for a long time in a cave on the Mount of Olives. The Moslems revere it as the tomb of still another lady: the mystic Rabi'a al Adawiyya.

During the fourth century we know that the very first episcopal residence (*episcopoi*, "inspectors," were the first leaders of the Christian community) was built on what today is Mount Zion. This name—which in Hebrew is connected with the concepts of "purpose," "election," and possibly means "chosen place"—has always been deeply evocative for the Jews. Originally it referred to Mount Ophel, then, as the city extended westward, it was also used for the second hill, which gradually usurped the name fully and is now its sole legitimate owner. Zion has also often been used to refer to Jerusalem as a whole (Ps. 48, 76, 87, etc.) and the expression "Bat Sion," "daughter of Zion," indicates the Jewish nation. It was here too, apparently, that Mark the Evangelist's house stood, and where the earliest meetings of Christians took place.

Another church, commemorating Christ's agony, was built near the garden of Gethsemane; but all that is left of it today are a few insignificant remains. It appears that at one point the Mount of Olives had at least twenty-five religious buildings on its slopes and on the sunny (and windy) expanse of its great crowning dome.

The fourth century was important both in the architectural development of the city and as regards monasticism and liturgy. Monasticism had its distant roots in certain groups of Jews (for instance, the Rechabites, and later the Essenes and "holy men" of Qumran) who had withdrawn from normal life in town and country and formed special isolated communities devoting themselves to strict discipline, study, ascetic practices, and a life of intense spirituality.

The lively interest in this new Christian Jerusalem that had succeeded Aelia Capitolina is shown by the number of pilgrims' accounts that have come down to our day. In 333—while Constantine's shrine was still being built—the holy places were visited by the Pilgrim of Bordeaux, who has left us an account of his journey. Shortly afterward it was the turn of Eusebius, Bishop of Vercelli (283–371), followed in 370 by St. Gregory of Nazianzus. Rufinus of Aquileia went there in 373 and the Spanish lady Etheria at the end of the century. In about 385 St. Jerome must have gone through Jerusalem and then settled in Bethlehem, where he spent over thirty years on intense literary, exegetic, and homiletic labors.

During the fifth century the Byzantine Emperor Theodosius II demonstrated his interest in the holy city several times; but it was mainly Queen Eudocia—a refugee from Byzantium, after terrible family intrigues ending in bloodshed—who devoted herself body and soul to embellishing the city with churches and monuments: it was she who inspired the founding of Santa Sophia of the Praetorium, of St.-Peter-of-the-Palace-of-Caiaphas, of St. John the Baptist (of which a small part remains in the form of a crypt), of a small church near the pool of Siloam, of the Martyrion of St. Stephen Without the Walls, to the north of the city, and of monasteries in various parts of Judaea. It was Eudocia, too, who rebuilt the walls of Jerusalem, so that the city

91

Church of St. Anne, interior

would not stand defenseless before the raids and invasions of the ever more threatening barbarians.

The great Golden Gate, rebuilt where there had originally been an older one (then known as the Susa Gate) between the Temple enclosure and the exterior, the valley of Josaphat, is often said to date from the time of Eudocia. This gate, kept firmly shut today, has a Byzantine colonnade on the interior, dividing the space into two naves; light falls from above, through the skylights of some small domes. The Byzantine architects took special care over its construction—inspired by the Golden Gate in Byzantium—because the edicule was to commemorate the curing of a paralytic by the apostles Peter and John (Acts 3) in front of the Beautiful Gate of the Temple. The lure of memory attracted other pious legends; from the sixth century the story went that this was the meeting place of Joachim and Anna, Mary's parents; from the eighth century onward this gate was identified with that through which Jesus entered the city during the festival of palms; and in the ninth century it was said that the Emperor Heraclius had gone through it with the remains of the true cross, after having taken it from the Persians, in his triumphal return to the holy city.

A passage from Ezekiel (44:2) also gave rise to the idea that one day the Messiah would enter Jerusalem through the closed Golden Gate. From the earliest times this idea particularly struck the Moslems, who barred the way with great walls and with a huge cemetery sprawling over the slopes of the hill, below the gate opposite Gethsemane ("the olive press"), a real minefield of the soul, to quote Alfred Bernheim, impassible because it could not be profaned.

Ever since Hadrian had decreed the destruction of Jerusalem, and since its rebuilding under another name as a center of the pagan world, Caesarea had been the capital of Palestine. This situation lasted for more than three hundred years. Church organization too, from the moment Christianity became the official state religion, had followed the administrative, giving Caesarea precedence over Jerusalem. But the time came when the city of the hill—bigger, more beautiful, walled once again, an unparalleled center of Christian life—could re-establish the just balance with the rival city; in A.D. 451 Jerusalem became the seat of the metropolitan patriarch, who had at least seventy bishops under his rule.

This happened precisely during the years when the West was tottering under the attacks of the Germanic peoples (Alaric besieged and took Rome in 410; the Vandals took and sacked it in 455). The contrast with the East, where peace and prosperity prevailed, was striking; and it seems that many refugees from the western peninsulas found welcoming refuge in calm and prosperous Palestine at this time.

With the reign of Justinian (527–565) the Eastern Empire once more had a moment of great splendor; an attempt—largely successful— was made to reconquer the lands lost in Italy, North Africa, and Spain. Jerusalem continued to grow in importance. Eudocia already had had a hostel built for the pilgrims who were arriving in increasing numbers; a few decades later St. Saba founded an important hospital for those who fell ill far from home. The number of the churches, shrines, monasteries,

92

and chapels scattered about Jerusalem and the surrounding countryside must have been amazing; we have information about many of them, a few remains of several. Not since the times of Solomon had the city looked so rich and splendid.

A mosaic plan of Jerusalem, discovered in 1897 at Madeba, gives a faint idea of the beauty of the city, while giving a very clear picture of its organic structure, which was later completely lost. The city was divided into two by a great avenue (Cardo Maximus) flanked by columns and probably by porticoes. Today a series of *suks*, covered markets, trace its course.

The centuries of flourishing Christian Jerusalem saw, in Asia, Africa, and Europe, an outburst, a tremendous burgeoning, of spiritual activity. The doctrines, organization, liturgy, and politics of a church—soon to be called Catholic, "universal"— were being formed and consolidated in a perennial battle against heretical, schismatic, subversive, reformist tendencies, by means of councils, synods, anathemas, apologias, treatises, and doxologies. All this was often linked with political, national, and class rivalries; in those days, people came out of academies, basilicas, and monasteries to enter the squares and indeed the battlefields.

The fortunes of Jerusalem were closely linked with those of Constantinople. As long as the Eastern emperors were able to keep Western Asia under control, all was well. Justinian had concluded a treaty of "perpetual peace" with the Persians, but this lasted only as long as the two empires could count on more or less equally balanced forces. When Justinian died the Eastern Empire went through a worrying period of weakening; but the Persians, under Chosroes II Parvez ("the Victorious"), felt more eager than ever to emulate the glories of the Achaemenids, whose heirs the Sassanid kings believed themselves to be. At the beginning of the seventh century Mesopotamia, Syria, some parts of Palestine, and Anatolia were invaded; soon Constantinople was threatened (609) and was saved only at the last moment by the skill of the strategist Heraclius. In the following years the Persians advanced through Armenia and Cappadocia, occupying Antioch, Damascus, Aleppo. The Greeks, though good administrators on the whole, had enemies in the Samaritans and Jews, and these, whenever possible, helped the Persians.

Jerusalem was besieged by the Persians in 614, and the episodes of similar previous operations were repeated: outside were the attackers bringing siege machines up against the walls, inside were the defenders putting up desperate resistance, while hunger weakened bodies and destroyed morale. The moment the Persians managed to make a breach in the walls (May 20, 614), the old and savage man hunt started up again through the streets and alleys of the city: men, women, children, and the old were mercilessly slaughtered. Contemporary sources speak of thirty-four thousand dead. The fury of the enemy, who had conquered a fortified city at a great price, was swelled by religious passion because many Jews who had followed the Persian army reveled in the fact that they were "liberating" the Christians' own city.

A double religious fanaticism—of Persians and Jews—encouraged not only the massacre of the inhabitants but also the destruction of the buildings. Everything was

93

Coenaculum, outer wall

shattered and reduced to ruins: the accumulated splendors of three hundred years disappeared at one blow, says Join-Lambert. Once again Jerusalem was reduced to the state she had known in 587 B.C. and A.D. 70. And, as before, all the inhabitants of any interest to the conquerors, either because they were noble or rich and able to pay ransoms, or craftsmen valued for their technical skills, were taken in chains into exile. Among the various treasures of the booty were also the relics of the cross.

The Persians held Jerusalem for a number of years (614–629). After the first and worst moments, the surviving Christians managed to gather up sufficient strength to make good the damage of the war, at least in part. Substantial help came from the Jewish Diaspora in Alexandria: they were able to rebuild the dome of the Anastasis and restore the basilica of the Martyrion. Many of the churches, particularly the majority on the Mount of Olives, remained in ruins. It was only after long preparation that the Emperor Heraclius (reigned 610–641) managed to muster up enough forces to beat the Persians (628); on March 21, 629, he re-entered Jerusalem, taking the relics of the cross, regained from his Eastern enemies, back to the Holy Sepulcher in triumph. (This day is celebrated there now as the Feast of the Cross.)

But the new Byzantine peace was to be very brief, enduring for only ten years, from 628 to 638. Meanwhile, in Arabia there had arisen a new and widespread movement founded by the prophet Mohammed, which was shortly to change the face of the known world.

94

XV | FROM THE SACRED MOSQUE TO
THE FARAWAY MOSQUE

The origins of the Jewish religion are lost in the mists of time, and it is hard to reconstruct them on the basis of documents which were composed far more recently than the facts they record. Even the beginnings of Christianity, so much nearer our own times, are confused, full of uncertainties and mystery. The traditional version, diluted and bowdlerized, gives us an idealistic and simplified picture: a Man appears who teaches and lays foundations, he is followed by various disciples who broadcast and convert. The facts collected by historical criticism, textual criticism, comparative study of religions, and archaeology present us with a doubtful, winding path, with strange bends and sudden changes, a seed falling to the ground and blossoming somewhere else, to bear fruit in yet a third place.

Everything is quite different concerning the origins of the third great religion born from the trunk of Abraham: Islam. Here, with a wealth of detail, we can follow the birth, first steps, temporary failure, and final victory of the new faith, which arose in the full noontide of history.

Mohammed was born in about 570 in Mecca, a center of pagan religious cults and an important stop for the caravans that provided communications between Yemen and Syria. After an infancy and youth made difficult and very probably painful by his having become an orphan at a very early age, we find Mohammed happily married to a rich widow, Khadija, whose business affairs he managed. In his capacity as trustee he apparently made various journeys to Syria.

We do not know much about Mohammed's education. It is most probable that as a child he was initiated into the cults of traditional Arab paganism and the already flourishing literature of his people. But other influences certainly acted upon him: there were large Jewish communities in the main cities of Yemen and Hejaz; Christian states—the Nestorian kingdom of Hira, the Monophysite one of Ghassan— bordered Arab territories to the north. Christian merchants, and possibly monks, often went as far as Arabia. Also, Mohammed's business travels may have put him in contact several times with both Jewish and Christian monotheists in their various orthodox and heterodox (Gnostic) versions, as well as their holy writings. There is a passage in the Koran (II, 248) that has led some authors to assume a direct and textual knowledge of at least part of the holy Judaeo-Christian books.

It is certain that Mohammed's spiritual life must have been particularly intense and characterized by deep meditation. His personality is one of the most complex in history; he combined the qualities of a mystic with those of a poet, the gifts of politician and warrior with a healthy taste for life in all its earthly manifestations.

Coenaculum, capital

Now we see him as leader of a city, a people, now as an adept and respected merchant, now as a general in arms, now as an incomparable poet and man of letters, now as a most understanding companion, husband, father; there is no imaginable human experience in which he did not participate with enthusiasm, passion, and vigor. We also know of his spiritual retreats *(tahannut)* into solitude. They preceded his most significant mystical experiences, those which finally led to the revelations, from the angel Gabriel, of the word deemed to be that of God.

Similar revelations, which succeeded one another for almost twenty years (probably from 610 until a little before his death in 632), were transcribed by friends and devout men on stone, palm leaves, polished animal bones, and other primitive surfaces. After the Prophet's death the various documents were collected together by his secretary Zaid ibn Tabit, and finally, under the Caliph Othman, about 650, there appeared the approved, official, and definitive version of the holy texts, later known as the Koran, i. e., "Recitation."

Several years after his first vision Mohammed began to spread his own ideas among his friends. At first he had few followers; indeed, the reactions of his fellow citizens became more and more hostile. As often happens, the Prophet found greater favor in a nearby town, Yathrib, where he took refuge and which was later known as Medinat en-Nabi (Medina), the "City of the Prophet."

This departure of Mohammed from Mecca (622) was known as the *Hijrah* (Hegira), often translated as "flight," a word quite unsuited to conveying the multiple meaning of the Arabic. *Hijrah* does have the sense of departure, migration, but it is also and essentially a precise legal term meaning "rescission of tribal ties." The Hegira marks a decisive moment in the life of Mohammed and his followers, when he detached himself from his own tribe to launch himself into an adventure that might go well, but might also end tragically. For an individual to break the links with his tribe meant, in those days, virtually to abandon himself to death: a group might survive if it managed to gain some kind of authority, but a lone man in the wild was doomed. Soon Mohammed was recognized as head of the city of Medina, and the fortunes of the new "people" soared. Instead of the customary tribal links, founded on blood, Mohammed instituted in Medina a community *(umma)* of believers.

There was also a big Jewish community in Medina. Mohammed saw his own mission as that of a last prophet, the spiritual descendant of those of the Old Testament, as well as of Jesus. But the Jews did not want to accept him among themselves, so Mohammed broke away from them completely.

The growing success of the Prophet and of his religion created new enemies and reinforced the hatred of the old. In 627 a confederation of tribes, about ten thousand men strong, besieged and was on the verge of taking Medina; Mohammed and his followers managed to save the city by fierce fighting. The Jews of Medina, who had tried to help the outside enemy, were almost all massacred or exiled. From this date onward the faithful of the Prophet grew steadily in power. A few years

96

Regaulpurg

later (632), upon Mohammed's death, a great part of Arabia was solidly in the hands of his followers.

Persia and Byzantium were exhausted after a long series of wars; when the time came to resist a new and powerful enemy from the south—the Arab people, who had found in Islam a new identity, a powerful unifying force—both revealed their own impotence; it was a positive collapse, which changed the pattern of the Middle East for ever. Ten years after Mohammed's death the Arabs had already conquered Syria and Egypt; a few years later (651) they strengthened their position in Persia; at the end of the century the Arab empire stretched from Spain to the gates of India. Not since the times of Alexander the Great had there been so thunderous a series of conquests. And it was not to be a short-lived affair. The present-day pattern in North Africa and the Middle East as far east as Pakistan largely reflects the events of these decisive decades.

In pitched battle, because of their extreme mobility, the Arabs had great tactical advantages over the heavily armed Byzantine and Persian soldiers, but they were unprepared for complex and prolonged siege warfare. Jerusalem, well protected by its circle of walls, remained free for some time, linked to Byzantium, when the remaining parts of Palestine and almost all of Syria had fallen into the hands of the Arabs. In 636 a decisive battle was fought at the river Yarmuk, to the east of Jordan, between the Byzantine forces under Theodore Sacellarius and the Arabs led by Abu Obeydah: the Arabs were the victors and had opened wide their way to the North.

Jerusalem was entrusted to the Patriarch Sophronius. As the Arabs advanced farther and farther he must have understood how useless it was to hope for Constantinople's recovery. After almost a thousand years passed in the sphere of the Hellenistic, Roman, and Byzantine world, Jerusalem was about to re-enter the sphere of the economic, cultural, and religious interests of Asia and the Semitic people.

In February 638 a small dark man (son of a Negress), poorly dressed, with the look of a wandering ascetic rather than that of a military leader, halted with an impressive army on the Mount of Olives: it was Omar, the second of the elective caliphs, the leader of Islam from 634 to 644. Patriarch Sophronius, having decided to negotiate with this new enemy, went to visit him. Most probably the good prelate went up the steep path to the mount with a sinking heart. He must have been greatly relieved when Omar told him his conditions: "In the name of Allah, the compassionate and merciful, this is the proclamation of Omar son of Khattab to the inhabitants of Bait al-Maqdis [the holy house]. Verily you are assured of the complete security of your lives, your goods, and your churches, which will not be inhabited nor destroyed by the Moslems, unless you rise up in a body...." Given the times, the Patriarch Sophronius could hardly have dreamed of a surrender negotiated in a more generous manner!

Entry into the Armenian quarter

After the formalities of the transfer, patriarch and caliph went off together to visit the city. The two men were just about to enter the Holy Sepulcher, when the hour of prayer was announced. The patriarch invited the caliph to pronounce it in the church itself, but the caliph declined the offer, pointing out that if he accepted the building would be considered sacred to Islam by his followers. He then stopped to pray in the atrium, which was in fact acquired by the Moslems later and where, in the tenth century, the small Mosque of Omar was built.

Later the caliph was taken by Sophronius to visit the esplanade where the great Temple of the Jews once rose, gleaming in the sun; this was also the site of the holy rock on which Abraham had prepared to sacrifice Isaac, and from which it was said that Mohammed ascended into heaven at the moment of a famous vision. After the destruction of the Temple by the Romans, the esplanade remained untended for centuries; except for very brief periods, the Jews had been excluded from the city, so that the place appeared simply as a deserted expanse of ruins. Throwing a handful of earth symbolically southward, Omar immediately embarked upon clearing the huge terrace of rubble; from that moment on the place became the property of the Moslems.

Shortly afterward a first mosque was built on the sacred rock—of wood, apparently, and very simple. Bishop Arculf (A.D. 670) described it as a square house of prayer, roughly built with beams and planks. It was not until later (between 685 and 691) that Caliph Abdul-Malik had the real Dome of the Rock built; and this, with only a few alterations, still survives and is one of the main monuments of Jerusalem, its greatest attraction.

Why were the Moslems so interested in Jerusalem? How did Jerusalem come to be the holy city for this third monotheist offshoot of the stock of Abraham? Mohammed never put himself forward as the founder of a religion without links with the past; in fact, he was much concerned to fit himself into the series of monotheist prophets, from Abraham to Moses, David to Jesus. At first he hoped that the Jews would accept him as an innovator within the sphere of traditional religion. At that time the *qibla*, the canonic direction one had to face when praying, was the north, that is, the direction of Jerusalem as seen from the Arabian peninsula. But when it proved impossible for Mohammed to fit into the line of the true Jewish religion, he changed the *qibla* and instructed the faithful to pray facing Mecca.

Jerusalem remained the city of the prophets, the great kings, the city of Jesus and Mary. Furthermore, Islamic traditions saw the Mount of Olives as the seat of the universal judgment, which Mohammed was to witness from the walls of the holy city. Finally, there was the old interpretation, advanced by Mohammed's immediate successors, of Sura 17 of the Koran, that of the "night journey"; this says, among other things: "Praise be unto him, who transported his servant by night from the sacred Mosque to the faraway Mosque...." This refers to the nocturnal ascent of the Prophet to the seventh heaven, where, led by an archangel, he was able to contemplate the divine face. Mohammed's successors interpreted the

98

phrase "faraway Mosque" (al-Aqsa) as meaning the esplanade of the Temple in Jerusalem, where the Prophet was said to have been taken by his mount al-Buraq (Lightning) and whence he ascended into heaven up a stairway actually starting from the rock of Abraham. This legend served to strengthen the deeply rooted belief that it was necessary, for an authentic prophet, to be hallowed by manifestations of divine favor on the holy ground of Jerusalem.

The new Moslem masters of the city gave proof of much tolerance. In any case Christians and Jews ("People of the Book") were regarded quite differently from idolaters. It is true that both these communities were gradually restricted by a series of special obligations, and their members deprived of some basic rights, so that they were in a sense second-class citizens: they had to pay more taxes than others; but beyond these limits they were not generally persecuted, and within these limits they could freely practice their professions and their faith.

The series of elective caliphs was followed by the hereditary dynasty of the Ommayad caliphs, with their center in Damascus (661–750). Later, under the Abbasid dynasty (750–1258), Baghdad was made the capital, and Jerusalem was administered as an important provincial city. Pilgrims of the time describe it as flourishing and populous, broadly tolerant of the special needs of residents and pilgrims belonging to so many different faiths.

About the end of the eighth century Byzantium—divided by religious and political struggles over the worship of images—no longer represented a danger to the Islamic states, which had developed economically and were going through a period of cultural splendor. In the West the power of the Franks was growing. Charlemagne, for both political and religious reasons, showed a lively interest in events in the East and sent important embassies to the court of the Caliph Harun al-Rashid.

Jerusalem felt the effects of these international developments. Many monuments and institutions connected with the Latin Church and its rites date back to the end of the eighth century and the beginning of the ninth. For more than a century Frankish protection and financing from the West helped to make the life of pilgrims and residents easier and safer. Then, gradually, this protection ceased. In the late tenth century (967) the Anastasis of the Holy Sepulcher was burned by enraged Moslems and Jews, and the current patriarch perished in the flames. For some decades it seemed that the Byzantine Empire, restored to strength under the Macedonian dynasty, might replace the Franks and protect the Christians in their distant outpost, but with the death of Nicephorus Phocas (969) the Byzantine military campaigns ceased without having affected Jerusalem. One important local result from the point of view of urban topography was this: the Moslems decided to reduce the walls to their present-day dimensions. The earlier walls ran around the slopes, even then sparsely populated, of Mount Ophel, down to the pool of Siloam; this was where the oldest cities had grown up, the Jerusalem of the Jebusites, of David, Solomon, even partly that of Herod, the Romans, the Byzantines. But gradually the inhabited

99

Theological seminary,
Armenian quarter

part had moved northward, from the steep uncomfortable slopes toward the plateau above them, where the Old City still has its center.

In about 1000 Jerusalem experienced some of the saddest moments in its long and tortured history. With the decline of the Abbasid dynasty various minor potentates held the fate of Palestine in their hands; at a certain point the Fatimids of Egypt (end of the tenth century) gained the ascendancy. The dynasty of the Fatimids—from Egypt and North Africa—was sectarian (Shiite) vis-à-vis orthodox Islam (Sunnite) and quite fanatical. From 996 to 1021 Jerusalem was under the rule of an intolerant and unrealistic visionary, the Fatimid Caliph al-Hakim, who devoted himself to a systematic destruction of the monuments of all faiths that were not his own. In 1009 the Holy Sepulcher was razed to the ground. Nothing now remained of the splendid buildings of Constantine; even the underlying rock was partly hacked out and carried away. A generation passed before it was possible to proceed, in the time of Emperor Constantine IX, Monomachus, with the partial reconstruction of the buildings that had been destroyed; the Martyrion was never restored, and the new architectural plan amounted to a complex of makeshifts, without anything of the logical unity of the old.

Hakim, meanwhile, had a curious destiny. He mysteriously disappeared in about 1021, and came to be regarded as a divine incarnation by the Druses, a dissenting new Islamic sect of whom about a quarter of a million still exist in the mountains of Israel, Syria, and Lebanon.

For several decades after the period of intolerance under Hakim, Jerusalem enjoyed another period of peace. The West was just beginning to wake up from its long sleep of the Middle Ages; the number of pilgrims increased yearly, indicating not only a vigorous sense of faith but a renewed vitality, a youthful curiosity regarding intellectual experiences beyond the narrow limits of a traditional horizon. In economic matters, too, old shackles were shaken off. The merchants of Amalfi, followed by others from Italian sea towns, were among the first to organize themselves; they succeeded in erecting important religious and civil buildings in Jerusalem near the Holy Sepulcher and in many other Eastern cities.

But momentous shifts of population were to change the map of Asia once again. For centuries the Turks had been pushing south and west from their original lands in Central Asia. In 1071 the Seljuk Turks won a great battle against Byzantine forces at Manzikert—one of the events that changed the course of history. It was then, in fact, that the Turks posed their candidacy for the conquest of Constantinople, which came about almost four centuries later under the Ottoman Turks.

Shortly after Manzikert the Seljuk Turks occupied Jerusalem (1077). The generally tolerant rule of the Sunnites, the rule of the Shiites which might or might not be fanatical, depending on the governor, was succeeded by a harsh, unyielding, bigoted regime. Pilgrims returned to Europe with alarming tales of almost unbearable taxes and general oppression.

Lane,
Armenian quarter

XVI | WHERE THE SOULS CONVENE

When an important architectural monument happens to be in a setting of great natural beauty, the effect is unforgettable. I am thinking of the temple at Segesta with its background of the stony mountains of Sicily brushed by the wind, the remains of the shrine of Poseidon high above the glittering sea of Cape Sounion, the cavernous vaults of the monastery of Ta-Phrom in the heart of the forest of Angkor beneath the monsoon rains—every reader can add other examples to the list, or make one of his own.

Jerusalem's Dome of the Rock has the sky.

After following a narrow alley in the Old City, winding its way between tall, irregular houses, a positive gorge sunk in shadow, filled with a shifting crowd and strings of patched washing hung in the air above, we cross the entrance known as Bab an-Nazir ("Gate of the Guardian"). Here we suddenly find ourselves gazing into blinding light, thrust into the blue, into free, clean space. The wind bends the green foliage of the sinewy-trunked cypresses, rolls along the odd scrap of paper, suddenly shortens the miniskirt of a brown-legged Nordic tourist.

A stairway of gleaming stone leads to the vast upper level where the Dome stands. My first sight of it made me think of mountaineering: there it stood, like an isolated peak glimpsed suddenly as one comes over the top of a glacier. It is a compact, harmonious building, marvelously aglow with color: it has the unchallengeable authority of a polyhedron set in a desert and at the same time the human warmth of a house. The gold of its dome shines in the sky, in the sun.

At the head of the staircase are typical four-arched arcades supported by columns with classical capitals: works which date mainly from the thirteenth and fourteenth centuries, the time of Saladin's brother Adil and the Mamelukes. "What a brain wave! How modern they are!" I heard someone near me in a group of French tourists exclaim. At first, one wonders whether these arches are not the remains of some building that was planned and only partly built. But the experts say that one can be quite certain that they were conceived precisely as they are, possibly to break up and limit the space, preparing the eye for the soaring spectacle of the Dome. They have the function of the Indian *torana,* the Chinese *p'ai-lou,* the *torii* in Japan; they frame, mark a border and an approach.

A few more steps, and we were at the foot of the Dome. Here everything seemed to conspire—nature, the work of man—to produce joy and serenity. The shape of the building, so absolutely definitive, might have been conceived to mark the world's center in space and to underline it for the eye of man. In fact this is one of the points

Steps leading to the Russian compound,
Ain Karem

of Jerusalem which ancient traditions regarded as the world's navel. The proportions of the building are marvelous; its placing in the landscape, perfect.

The sky is the great protagonist. Peerless blue, or lightly plumed with clouds, or furrowed with the wakes of high-flying jets, it is both a background and a living thing. The walls of the Dome, with their facing of green and blue tiles, prepare the eye for its journey toward the blue, the steeping of the building in the sky, its wedding with space. Above is the golden blaze of the dome itself. Its present covering is very recent (1960). Anyone not in Jerusalem, reading in a book or magazine that this is composed of layers of gilded aluminum, will curl his lip and think: Yet another piece of modern barbarism. But one must admit that the tone is absolutely perfect: it is gold, certainly, but without a brazen glitter, an opaque gold which reflects the sun's splendor with diffused gentleness. I think that a Japanese would here use the word *shibui* (austere good taste). In fact it has the tone of the antique gold on the backgrounds of the screens and *fusuma* (sliding doors) in the temples of Kyoto.

Visitors and pilgrims from all over the world approach singly, in couples, or in groups. The differences, apart from the indelible ones of hair and skin, now seem more noticeable between the various ages than the various nations. Today the world appears divided into chronological strata rather than spatial islands. Different ideas of male and female beauty, of dress, indeed of undress, of hair styles, of ways of eating, dancing, amusing oneself, relaxing or making love, divide young from old of all latitudes. American, Israeli, German, Arab, Japanese, African boys and girls all have something in common: but as soon as you move upward in age groups toward that of the older brothers or parents, you see the Yank reappearing in the American, the Nippon in the Japanese, the Gaulois in the French. The worthy fifty-year-old pilgrims in buses are identifiable on a positively regional basis: you can distinguish Bretons from Bavarians, Sardinians from Texans, Midlanders from natives of Navarre. But let us not delude ourselves: the young people of today, like those of all time, gradually move back toward their traditional molds as they grow older. Ultimately a step forward will have been taken, but certainly a smaller one than one might imagine from looking at sandals and beards, guitars and duffel bags.

Approaching the Dome, the eye is drawn by the glazed tiles of the outer walls as if by a field in flower. Succulent cobalts are wedded to vibrant greens; here and there are knowing touches of yellow and restful empty spaces. Mostly, the minute, precise design of the swirls stands out from a luminous white background which continues that of the marble covering the base. There is both the power of certain explosions of color of a Pollock and the subtle geometries of a Mondrian.

Higher up, above a series of seven arches on each side, and above two bands of geometrical friezes, is a strip of Arabic inscriptions in elegant white characters against a blue background. Verses from the Koran, I was told.... Unfortunately, all I could admire was the filigree of lines. Every system of writing creates its own aesthetic. None, I think, will ever be able to outdo the fascination of Chinese and Japanese ideograms simply because of the enormous variety of the symbols and their combinations, which continually produce new balances, almost all dynamic and asymmetrical. The eye follows them one by one as if they were performing a dance on the paper. In contrast, one might think of Nepalese or Tibetan scripts, with their obsessive repetition of vertical lines whose accumulation gives the page the look of a piece of embroidery. Arabic writing, particularly the sinuous, graceful writing of the time of Suleiman the Magnificent, stands halfway between the two; it has sufficient variety to make one aware of the unfolding of a graphic counterpoint, while on the other hand the prevalence of vertical lines accentuates its bold vertical assertion. Beside these fascinating symphonies of symbols, how poor and unimaginative are the Roman, Greek, and Cyrillic scripts! From the aesthetic point of view, I would say that the lowest rung of the ladder is left to the Hebrew: it is as though its lines are in a perpetual state of hesitation as to their own identity—are they horizontal? vertical? oblique? Furthermore, the variety of the symbols is limited, the words fail to group themselves into definite graphic organisms. Perhaps the importance of what was being said was such that subdued dress was more becoming? Or was it a congenital indifference to the beautiful?

The facing of the outer walls is of tiles from Kashan, in Persia, dating from about 1545. Before that, apparently, there were mosaics; the building must have looked far more Byzantine then than it does today. At the time of the Moslem conquest, it seems that a wooden structure surmounted the rock of Abraham. This emerges from the writings of Archbishop Arculf, who visited Jerusalem in 670 and whose account of his journey was widely read in the Middle Ages. A few years later (687 to 691) the Ommayad Caliph Abdul-Malik built the noble building which has survived virtually intact until today. Abdul-Malik was prompted as much by political as by religious motives: he wished to counteract on the one hand the architectural impact of the Christian dome of the Sepulcher in Jerusalem's skyline, with a Moslem dome, and on the other hand the cult of the Black Stone in Mecca by that of Abraham's rock, so that Jerusalem, held by him, should gain in importance as against Mecca, which was in the hands of his rival Ibn Zobair.

If you wish to visit the interior you have to remove your shoes. An imposing battery of shoes of all kinds, sizes, and colors is arrayed outside the doors. Attendants even provide slippers for those who want them, but many enter barefoot, and anyhow this is fashionable today, particularly among the young. The moment you pass through the entrance your eyes are struck with new splendors, while your nose, less fortunate, is plunged into air that smells old and stale, well seasoned with an essence of feet not too familiar with soap and water. Breathing becomes a trial, and you have to condemn your lungs to an austerity diet.

If outside was a universe of light and simplicity, here is an empyrean of shadow and ornament. On the floor, carpets the color of congealed blood are lit up here and there by rays of sun which fall, like flaming meteorites, from the high, brightly colored, stained-glass windows. Looking upward, one's gaze hesitates amid a delirium of lines, colors, patterns. The internal space is divided concentrically by two orders of columns and arches, an outer octagonal and an inner circular; they frankly reveal the structure of the building and underline the varying functions of its parts. Faithful and visitors alike stroll around it on the outside; inside, at the center, protected by a balustrade of the twelfth century, stands the rock of Abraham.

The ground plan of a circular building immediately brings to mind, like a Tibetan mandala, an attempt at cosmological representation. The idea would be singularly appropriate for a building placed on a point of such cosmic importance: center of the world, launching platform for extraterrestrial voyages. Ramón Lull in his *Ars Magna* hints at three concentric circles as "containers of all the mysteries," but it may be a coincidence. Of the many religions that have flourished among men, eighth-century Islam, before the appearance of the great mystics, must have been one of the least sensitive to those hints of metaphysical harmonies linking macro- and micro-cosm.

The mosaics on the arches supported by the octagonal colonnade are the oldest, dating from the eighth century. They contain a marvelous complex of highly stylized palms, trunks, branches, flowers, leaves, fruits, garlands, and jewels. The Byzantine influence is clearly in evidence. We are in a supremely anti-anthropomorphic world, where nature has lost all independence and spontaneity, being reduced to a geometrical network of things imprisoned in their own forms. I was struck by how differently a similar space would be decorated in the Far East, where nature is not something inert or passive, to be used or dominated, but an infinite and mysterious organism with which man would be wise to seek some kind of agreement. In the decoration, for instance, of the Nishi Hongwan-ji of Kyoto, trees, flowers, branches, and stones overrun the walls at random, without respecting even the architectural framework; they are spontaneous nature with which man feels he can ally himself as a brother.

But here speculation is a luxury: the insidious stink of feet penetrates your nose, your tracheae. I had thought I was getting used to it, but it actually seemed to be getting worse every minute. In the middle of the building stands the great limestone rock which was once supposedly the tip of the hill of Moriah. It is a great blond slab with a dense, pitted surface; it looks like the summit of a Dolomite mountain lifted intact and deposited right in the heart of Jerusalem. Beneath it is a cave lit by electric light—where, according to a pious Islamic belief, the souls of the dead gather to sing their inaudible praises of Allah. You reach this cave by a little stairway. Here the stale air is closer than ever, with an even greater proportion of the distinctive element in it; it is to be hoped that, apart from living on a level all their own as far as sight and hearing are concerned, the souls of the dead are also cut off from our lowly world in their sense of smell.

All around hover myths, historical memories, legends. One thinks of Abraham with his knife raised above the neck of his child. He is about to deliver the fatal blow when the voice comes down from above: "Lay not thine hand upon the lad,

104

Russian compound,
Ain Karem

neither do thou anything unto him, now I know that thou fearest God" (Gen. 22:12). And then there is the expert touch of the Biblical storyteller: "And Abraham lifted up his eyes, and looked, and behold behind him a ram caught in a thicket by his horns...." Here the highly dramatic and moving episode ends. It had begun shortly before when Isaac—who obviously had not been told anything of the sacrifice the Lord demanded—asked his father: "Behold the fire and the wood, but where is the lamb for a burnt offering?" Abraham answers: "My son, God will provide himself a lamb for a burnt offering." The reader gets the impression that Abraham is inventing an excuse, feeling unable to tell his son the truth. When the ram appears in the bush all falls into place, the whole episode acquires the perfection of a cameo.

One may also think with pleasure of Ornan, owner of this windy spot at the time of King David. Perhaps he kept straw for the animals and agricultural implements in the cave. Here the most humble and homely things come together with the most august and celestial. As when, precisely here, Mohammed took flight for his secret experiences in paradise. According to a pious legend, the rock itself, suddenly freed from its material gravity, was going to follow the Prophet, but the angel Gabriel was able to keep it in place with one hand. The imprint of his hand is still—so they say—shown to pilgrims. Unfortunately, my guide, either because he was in a hurry to escape the smell or because he thought an infidel would have little understanding of these things, omitted to show it to me.

At last we re-emerged into the open. It was marvelous to breathe the air blowing in from the countryside, bending the tips of the tall sunlit cypresses. We walked all around the Dome. To the east stands the odd but graceful chapel known as the Dome of the Chain *(Qubbat es-Silsileh)*. Here too the facing of glazed tiles dates from the time of Suleiman; the capitals of the columns are Byzantine. Once treasure was stored here, for the complete visibility of every approach guaranteed security.

Walking over the huge esplanade of the Haram is one of the greatest pleasures to be had in Jerusalem. It is in absolute contrast to the other: wandering among the crowd, observing, watching, mingling, at the Gate of Damascus, in the *suk,* on the small square of the Jaffa Gate, in the Christian holy places, near the Jewish western wall of the Temple. They seem two worlds completely separate and distinct: in the one there is space, silence, and sky; in the other, crowds, chaos, contrast of darkness with rays of light. On the esplanade there are a number of small shrines of greatly varying shape and nature, each with its own architectural importance. Particularly fascinating is the fountain of Qait Bey (1482), both for the warm color of its stone and for certain ingenious solutions of structural and decorative problems, kept closely interlinked.

On the Haram there are some parts one might call gardens, others where olive trees are growing which look like little patches of open country. Walking eastward, one comes to the Golden Gate (now closed and difficult to visit) and the highest, most powerful part of the walls, which had looked so impressive from below, from the valley of Kedron. Toward the south a spacious covered gallery follows the interior

Russian compound, garden,
Ain Karem

of the walls and enables one to reach the pinnacle of the mount. Those who do not mind heights can climb onto the battlements and have a spectacular view. Far below lies the valley of Kedron, with the village of Silwan (the Biblical Siloam) to the right. Directly in front there are several great tombs; the most noticeable, dating from the Hellenistic era, is known (on a "history-fiction" level) as the tomb of Absalom. Above and right in front is the Mount of Olives, scattered with Jewish tombs of every period.

The Mount of Olives is no longer what it once was, as it appeared in nineteenth-century prints: a lonely place where one could wander and meditate. Today, if one were to name it after the objects most conspicuous on its slopes, it should be called the Mount of Hotels. And through the valley of Kedron, where according to traditions common to the three monotheistic religions the trumps of the angels will one day sound to gather humanity for the last judgment, one hears the perpetual jarring honking of the trumps of cars and buses.

But none of this matters. The view is still marvelous. Amid floods of sun and bursts of wind, you can spend hours thinking about the things these stones must have seen: from the war engines of the Romans to those of the Persians, from Emperor Heraclius, who restored the relics of the true cross to Jerusalem, to the tanks which fought in the Six-Day War of 1967. Then, when you are tired, or are bothered by the sun, you can easily go down one of the little flights of steps, under the terrace, to what are known as Solomon's stables. They are huge underground vaults, mainly of a much later date (Herod and Justinian). The floor is of a dusty yellowish-gray earth; the occasional whiff of rather suspect odor leads one to believe that many profit from a few moments' solitude down here to rid themselves of superfluous corporeality.

Going out into the open again, turning west, we come to the Mosque of al-Aqsa, with its silver dome. It is certainly not as beautiful as the Dome of the Rock, but it has a sober nobility. At first sight one might think that it is a basilica transformed into a mosque. But the artistic history of the monument tells us that this is not so. What happened was that, in time, all buildings approached nearer and nearer to the type of the basilica. Solomon's palace probably stood here, approached from the valley of Kedron—then within the circle of the walls—by means of a gate, probably beneath the later Herodian Double Gate, now walled up. After the Moslem conquest apparently a refuge was built here for the faithful, making use of some ruins that stood on the spot; the real mosque was built only between 709 and 715 under the Omayyad Caliph al-Walid, the son of the Caliph Abdul-Malik, the builder of the Dome of the Rock, and restored and extended after an earthquake under the Abbasid Caliph al-Mahdi, about 780.

With the passing of time, with wars and earthquakes, the old building underwent considerable and continuous transformations. The Latin kings and Templars (who took their name from this holy place) left their traces. Finally two unexpected characters of recent history, Mussolini and King Farouk of Egypt, came to give the

106

finishing touches to the appearance of the building, one contributing the columns, of Carrara marble, which make up the skeleton of the interior, the other the great beams of the ceiling.

The interior of the mosque is full of light, like some huge refectory for virgins. Arabic inscriptions in circles stand out from the white of the walls, intriguing as seals. Beneath the dome there are mosaics dating from the time of Saladin; colors and motifs are reminiscent of the mosaics of Palermo. They remind one of the cultural unity of the Mediterranean at the time of the Norman kings and Emperor Frederick II.

The *mihrab* (niche toward which the faithful turn in prayer, which indicates the direction of Mecca) is most beautiful, as is the twelfth-century *minbar* (pulpit) of carved wood. Jerusalem has been despoiled too often throughout the centuries for works any more fragile than an arch or a wall to have survived. Furthermore, fanaticism, indeed sometimes iconoclastic frenzy, stifled any real growth of the figurative arts. The visitor's eye and hand pause with particular delight on these subtle geometries carved in the centuries-old ebony.

Portal of the Ethiopian cathedral

XVII | "DEUS LE VOLT!"

The West was now going through a period of recovery. In Spain the task of reconquest had begun and the Almoravides were losing ground fast. Papacy and Empire, ready to cross swords when it was a question of internal European affairs, were solidly organized and could join forces against a common enemy. A young emperor of Byzantium, Alexius Comnenus, despairing of ever being able to drive the Turks from Anatolia and Syria on his own, turned to Pope Urban II for help, at least in manpower, if not in arms and money.

This was the origin of a series of military enterprises known as the Crusades, which, on the one hand, put up a Christian and Western armed response to the Islamic and Oriental jihad (holy war), and on the other brought about a broadening of geographical and cultural horizons valuable for both Europe and Asia. The period was to alter the shape and appearance of Jerusalem profoundly, giving it most of the features the visitor sees today.

The attitude to war, as Sir Steven Runciman observes in his masterful history of the Crusades, was very different in the two worlds of Christendom, East and West. The first, in accordance with the old anathema against violence uttered by St. Basil, accepted war as a necessary evil but did not crown the soldier with a halo of glory. The West, where St. Augustine had already sanctioned the lawfulness of wars undertaken for a holy end, where the ruling class consisted mainly of Nordic men of warrior stock, gradually came to idealize men of arms and warlike exploits to a disproportionate degree; there was a positive mystique regarding the warrior and the knight, of which there are traces in the European mind even today. Popes such as Leo IV and John VII promised heavenly rewards to those who died in battle in defense of the Church, and under any circumstances if fighting the infidel.

When Pope Urban II, at the Council of Clermont (1095), launched the idea of a great popular armed rising of all of Europe to free the holy places of Palestine from the dominion of "the infidel," the response was immediate and enthusiastic. Not only did shouts of *"Deus le volt"* ("God wills it") break into the Pope's very words, but within a few months in almost all the countries of Europe groups of armed men were formed, ready to leave on a voyage which, given the times and means of communication, would have to be undertaken with great and serious care.

Unfortunately, this call to arms and adventure—launched in highly emotional terms, in cruel and superstitious times—attracted not only dreamers and idealists but also many people who envisaged easy and rapid material gain. Furthermore, the tone of religious fanaticism roused all the dormant barbarity of the Western psyche, and "the Crusade" led the warriors to extend their anger, firstly, to many communi-

108

Women's quarters,
Ethiopian compound

ties of Jews who had been living more or less peacefully in European cities: Worms, Mainz, Cologne, Trier, and Metz were stages in a grim series of violence and massacre.

A vanguard of people of the most diverse origins, ill armed and without any organization except a childish enthusiasm, led by the strange figure of clown-*cum*-mystic Peter the Hermit, ended disastrously. The more serious First Crusade, organized by the Frankish and Norman barons, proceeded slowly toward its goal amid internal disagreements and quarrels with the Emperor Alexius. The Turks were defeated at Dorylaeum (1097); Edessa was conquered, Antioch was taken after a year of siege (1098). Another year passed and the crusading forces, reckoned at between twelve and thirteen thousand men, saw the distant walls of Jerusalem for the first time.

"The city of Jerusalem was one of the great fortresses of the medieval world," says Runciman. It had been taken from the Turks shortly before by the Fatimids of Egypt; and it was from them that the Crusaders had to wrest it. The commander of the fortress, the Governor Iftikhar ad-Dawla, had strengthened the defenses powerfully and was in charge of a large force, with good supplies of food and water. The siege began on June 7, 1099. A few days later (June 12) the Crusaders, spurred on by the words of a hermit, launched a first assault but were repulsed. In the following weeks they worked at top speed to prepare siege machines; work was halted only for a solemn procession around the walls of the city, in accordance with the orders of Bishop Adhemar, recently dead, given in a dream to the priest Desiderius.

At last the siege machines were ready. On July 14, 1099, the attack was launched. At first resistance seemed strong, almost impossible to break down, but at midday on July 15 the first Crusaders managed to set foot on the walls, leaping onto them from one of the great wooden towers. Several of the boldest men then rushed to open the northern gates, and soon the city was overrun. The defenders tried to take refuge on the Haram-ash-Sharif, but they did not have the time to raise fortifications. Iftikhar himself surrendered, offering Raymond of Toulouse, the ranking Crusader, a large sum of money in exchange for his life.

Raymond let the enemy commander leave with his men. For the others, the Jews and Moslems who remained in the city, hours of terror were at hand. The soldiers of the cross, "maddened by so great a victory after such suffering," tore wildly through the streets killing men, women, and children indiscriminately. The bloodbath went on throughout the evening and night; the next morning the soldiers forced their way into the Mosque of al-Aqsa, and all those who had taken refuge in it were slaughtered. As for the Jews, held guilty of having helped the Moslems to resist, they were burned alive inside their main synagogue, where they had taken shelter.

The massacre of Jerusalem carved a rift between Christians, Moslems, and Jews which was to remain deep for centuries. The number of victims was estimated at about thirty thousand; it seems that the city was virtually emptied of its former

Church of the Holy Sepulcher

inhabitants. With their swords still dripping with "infidel" blood, we read in the chronicles of the time, the Crusaders marched in solemn procession to the Holy Sepulcher to thank God for their victory, which is celebrated even now by the Latin Patriarch of Jerusalem annually on July 15.

The conquest of Jerusalem, despite many difficulties, had succeeded under what we today would call "corporate management." Then the barons gathered in Jerusalem elected Godfrey of Bouillon as their ruler; he modestly took the title of "Defender of the Holy Sepulcher," refusing to wear a crown of gold "in the city where Christ had worn a crown of thorns."

On Godfrey's death (1100) he was succeeded by his brother Baldwin I, who was crowned at Jerusalem on Christmas Day, 1100. An energetic, ambitious, and unscrupulous man, in a few years he managed to consolidate the Crusaders' conquests into a real state. New conquests by Baldwin II (reigned 1118–1131), who succeeded him, took the frontiers of the kingdom to their maximum extent. A Moslem counteroffensive, which could not but be long in coming, first made itself felt during the reign of Fulk I (1131–1144) and Queen Melisende, when Imad ed-Din, prince of Aleppo, favored a decisive policy of reunion of the Moslem world. King Fulk managed to ally himself with the emir of Damascus, and thus for some time kept his greatest adversary in check.

By now the Frankish barons, especially those of the second generation, born overseas, had adapted themselves to the altogether different conditions of life in the new country. They had also cleverly entered into the political game of the Levant. In some ways a mutual tolerance was growing up between Christians and Moslems, which offered hope for the future.

After his accidental death, Fulk was succeeded by his son, a minor, Baldwin III, under the regency of Queen Melisende. The Turks took advantage of the situation to reconquer the city of Edessa. In Europe there was great consternation, and a second Crusade was organized, which had very limited effects. Amalric (reigned 1162–1173), who succeeded his brother Baldwin, fought against Turks and Egyptians and kept the kingdom of Jerusalem within its traditional boundaries for a decade.

During this period the dream of Moslem unity inspired a man of exceptional valor and brilliance: Salah ed-Din Yusuf (Saladin). His career as a leader began when he united Islamic Egypt and Syria, leaving Christian Jerusalem in the middle, isolated. In vain the leprous young King Baldwin IV tried to resist the enemy. The final disaster took place under Guy de Lusignan, when the Franks lost the crucial battle of the Horns of Hattin (1187). Jerusalem was taken by Saladin shortly thereafter, though without a repetition of the massacres of 1099.

In the decades that followed, the Crusaders made numerous attempts to return to Jerusalem. A third expedition (under Richard Cœur de Lion) never reached its goal. Emperor Frederick II was more skillful, and managed, by peaceful means, to make an agreement with the Moslems: this gave him a sort of shared rule over Jerusalem which lasted for at least fifteen years (1229–1244).

110

XVIII | STILL BRAVELY ALIVE

The Dome of the Rock and the Holy Sepulcher stand at opposite poles of every conceivable world. The first is towering, solitary, steeped in the blue and the clouds; the second is buried in the bowels of the city where all that can be seen of the sky is little irregular patches between the roofs, walls, minarets, and bell towers. The former is the fruit of a single-minded conception; the second is one of the most complicated architectural, stylistic, and chronological jumbles on the face of the earth. The first is based on simple geometrical forms; the second is a sort of geology of metamorphic stratifications shattered by the earth's heavings. The first is elegant and pure; the second, clumsy and hybrid. The first inspires joy in the heart at its very sight; the second is depressing, dismal. The first is a hymn; the second, a groan.

Despite all this, perhaps because of it, time spent in, near, or around the Holy Sepulcher is meaningful. Here is the usual problem: among men, with whom do your sympathies lie, the conquerors or the conquered in life? Architecturally speaking, the Holy Sepulcher is one of the conquered; indeed crushed, shattered, ground down. The walls bear sixteen centuries of grief on their flesh of stone, its doors are ill-healed wounds, its walls lean and creak with some equivalent to rheumatism, its innards are swollen, its limbs are in place only thanks to complicated prostheses. Furthermore, if in the Dome of the Rock one's thoughts turn naturally to a rather mysterious and distant God, vibrating in the universe in some subtle, electric way, who perhaps created us in error, or in jest, or because he had nothing else to do that afternoon, in the Holy Sepulcher we are involved in a drama which bathed the earth in blood and shook the heavens, where talk is of sin and forgiveness, mother and son, love and suffering: the universe is no longer a starred vault over the wilderness, but a heart, a womb, hands tortured by nails. Here the meeting point in space is much less important than that in time: incarnation, passion, death, redemption, are the real umbilical events in the oceans of time.

I sat down on a stone bench not far from the entrance to the Holy Sepulcher. It was a summer morning. The sun shone on the little square, half cluttered up by a shed where masons were preparing stones for restoration work. The façade of the church too was largely covered with scaffolding and trestles. People of every possible aspect walked by me: two pale Armenian priests with goatees and tall triangular hoods (called "Ararat" after the famous Armenian mountain), a group of French pilgrims, American hippies, Franciscan friars, an old man with a fez, a Negro family, Israeli soldiers with submachine guns slung over their shoulders, fair girls with long sunburned legs bare virtually to the crotch, heavily muffled nuns, a Coptic priest;

III

Church of St. Simeon,
Katamon quarter

then a young man with a tray balanced on his head holding rows of loaves fresh from the oven. He was certainly not off to peer into the loculi in Joseph of Arimathea's tomb with a flashlight, as most of the tourists would be doing; I imagined he was off to the bakeshop around the corner. A complete gamut of human activities and accessories—the voices of the masons at work, oranges and holy pictures in an old woman's basket, the coins a guide was counting after having shown around some tight-fisted pilgrims, bread, cigarette butts, bottles of Coca-Cola—ascends to the most sublime, Mary, Christ himself, where flesh is a bridge between man and universe. Indeed, perhaps the ultimate fascination that Christianity has exerted over so many peoples throughout so many centuries has been, and is, this: that the great leap between ourselves and the unknowable does not take place in the abstract, but in the concrete, in the form of a drama whose core is suffering and death, followed by resurrection and light.

The Holy Sepulcher today is a building that has lived through earthquakes, fires, centuries of elemental and human violence. It is only too easy to compare it to the old trunk of a mountain tree, twisted and knotted, but still bravely alive.

The first disaster took place less than three centuries after Constantine's architects had completed the basilica of the Martyrion and the rotunda of the Anastasis (Resurrection). This was in 614. When they occupied Jerusalem, the Persians set fire to its holy buildings. Soon afterward the Patriarch Modestos managed to repair what was left standing. Another three centuries passed. In about 1000 the Caliph Hakim, seized with a mad fanaticism, embarked upon a regime of persecution; in 1009 he actually had the buildings of Constantine's era demolished, claiming that the so-called miracle of the lighting of the fire, which took place (as it still does) on Easter Saturday, must have been a piece of impious magic. His men not only destroyed walls and arches, columns and roofs, but apparently demolished the rock where Jesus' tomb was. "The last trace of the natural state of the site was obliterated," says André Parrot. Only the little hill of Golgotha (also called Calvary) was respected. Some years later the Anastasis was rebuilt after a fashion on the orders of the Eastern Emperor Constantine Monomachus. The Martyrion remained a heap of ruins, and its place may already have been taken by other buildings.

When the Crusaders occupied Jerusalem (1099), they immediately wanted to rebuild the Holy Sepulcher. They could have adopted the plans used in the age of Constantine, but this seemed too large-scale an undertaking. So instead they decided completely to rebuild the Anastasis, then to build a church behind it which would occupy the space where the atrium between the Martyrion and Anastasis had originally been. This church was not to be as long as the original basilica, but much broader, and was to take in under its roof all that remained of the original Golgotha. In this way all three holy places—Jesus' tomb, Golgotha, and the cave of the cross— would be brought together in a single building. Work went on for half a century (1099–1149) but the result, as might have been foreseen, was a strange hodgepodge. The church, which has obvious elements of the Burgundian Romanesque, has no

112

nave, only the transept, choir, and apse; the latter is surrounded by an ambulatory with chapels opening off it. From the original foundation onward, therefore, we are plunged into architectural teratology; subsequent centuries made this architectural medley still more incongruous by inserting doors, putting up walls, dividing and subdividing in accordance with fanatical and shortsighted sectarianism. Today, luckily, bold and large-scale restorations are giving the building back some of the lines and appearance intended for it by the Frankish masters.

The Crusaders also built a big bell tower. It lost its topmost story in 1549, and has been capped with a roof of red tiles since 1719. Its original bells rang only until 1187, when Saladin—while respecting the rest of the building—had them destroyed. Now there are bells again, but their ringing may not interfere with the call of the muezzin.... There were violent earthquakes in 1545, 1927, and 1937. There were fires, the worst one in 1808 and the latest in 1949, and there were wars. Lastly, there was often the scourge of masons who created and destroyed at their own whim, for instance the Greek architect Komnenos Kalfa who persisted with his pointless innovations in the early years of the nineteenth century.

Before 1000 the buildings of the Holy Sepulcher had two entrances: one was the monumental one to the east, opening onto the Cardo and little square in front of the Martyrion; the other was a sort of short cut direct to the Anastasis, to the south. The Crusaders, eliminating the reconstruction of the Martyrion from their plans, did away with the eastern entrance. The second, the southern one, thus became the main entrance. But since they had aligned their church roughly the same as the Martyrion had been, the new entrance appears somewhat meanly treated. In reality the present façade is structurally a side wall of the building, which adds other, unforeseen elements of confusion to the picture.

I gazed at the façade. The lovely golden color of the stone, the projecting stones of the arches above doors and windows, so similar for instance to that on the bell tower of the Martorana in Palermo, made me think of Sicily. The knights and abbots may have been Franks or Normans, but the craftsmen were probably from Sicily or Puglia; the cultural unity of the Mediterranean throughout that whole period must have been a tangible reality. It is an interesting fact that the arches are pointed. As is well known, many experts believe that this building method is of Arab origin, even though it became so typical of a northern European style, the Gothic.

Above the two entrances (one is walled up) there were once Romanesque bas-reliefs, now in the Jerusalem Rockefeller Museum. They have a delightfully immediate appeal: the first shows, in succession, the raising of Lazarus, Jesus' triumphal entry into Jerusalem, and the last supper, while the other is ornamental, though human figures intertwined with branches and plants reveal an unsuspected pagan joy in the representation of young men's bodies. Originally, it seems, there were mosaics in the tympana, but these have completely disappeared.

Just inside the door is a dark, drafty passage where visitors are shown a slab of reddish limestone on which, according to the Latins, Christ's body was embalmed,

Church of the Nativity,
Bethlehem

while according to the Greeks it was placed there when he was taken down from the cross. On one side, sitting on a folding camp stool, I noticed an elderly lady dressed in a sort of nun's habit and rough sandals, deeply absorbed in sketching on a block of paper. I had noticed her a few days earlier on the Mount of Olives. She was blonde, with a purple ribbon in her hair, one of a whole world of foreigners, somewhere between the mystical and the artistic, who are drawn by the lure of this strange city, as others are drawn by Florence, Benares, Kyoto.

A few steps to the left, and you are in a passage which leads into the actual rotunda of the Sepulcher. It is a great, gray, gloomy well. To say that it is reminiscent of a huge hall in a railway station, with a pretentious catafalque placed somewhat unceremoniously in the middle, would by no means give the whole picture. It should be added that it is a railway station propped up by all manner of reinforcements. Above, a remote ceiling, damp and peeling, is set on walls supported by awkward stone pillars. Enormously thick iron tie bars suggest a stability threatened by earthquakes, fires, and bombs. It is not a colonnade but a racklike construction put up when metallurgy had reached the stage of the Eiffel Tower.

I must admit that I had not expected anything quite so hideous, even though we live in post-Christian times, as Toynbee says. The abysmal state of the place is particularly surprising when one considers that the people who provide the greatest number of pilgrims are not the most deprived on earth.

But Christianity is divided. The new ecumenical breezes scarcely move the heavy, unwieldy old ship. Here disunity is noticeable on a more sordid and grotesque level in the rivalries between Greek and Latin, Syrian and Armenian, Copt and Ethiopian. It is like being in a kitchen, where groups of cooks belonging to different and rival branches of a huge family find themselves brought together for a wedding or funeral and spite one another in a most childish way: The ladle? I don't know, it may have fallen in with the rubbish. Vinegar? I've just spilled it all.... Meanwhile on the floors above the guests and givers of the party thrust mortal blows at one another with secret contracts or pretended transactions. This is what goes on in the house of Christ! And high up, on metaphysical and esoteric, curial or conciliar levels, the fight continues with thrusts of filioque or thelema, justification or infallibility, predestination or free will, unleavened or leavened bread, with shouts of long live Nestorius or long live Pelagius, long live Luther or long live Barth, long live the Pope or long live the Patriarch. But down here it is fencing with brooms, counting candles, drops of oil, inches of bench. Every creed has its frontiers in the great well, old but still disputed, following illogical, elusive lines. Professionals in religion stand on guard, mostly uncouth and greasy, in priestly garb of various kinds, spying on their rivals' every movement. The simple act of sweeping or cleaning a stretch of the church, if permitted, could set precedents for subsequent occupations.

In the center of the building is the actual chapel of the tomb, defined even by André Parrot as a "frightful kiosk." Rather than a cenotaph, it is reminiscent of a

114

Church of the Nativity, interior,
Bethlehem

wedding cake in variously colored marble, erected from scratch in one of the least happily inspired artistic periods (1809), surrounded by hanging oil lamps, over-burdened with ornaments, holy images, ex-votos, other showy manifestations of popular piety. Inside are two minute cells, one known as the angel's cell, housing a piece of the stone where, according to tradition, the angel of the Resurrection alighted; the second, smaller still—you have to bend almost double to enter—which is supposedly the real tomb. But as we have seen, the repeated demolitions and radical changes throughout the centuries render a positive identification of the place purely illusory.

A crowd of people of all ages, colors, types, and tongues pauses in front of the little shrine; almost all of them allow themselves to be led right into the two cells, brightly lit by bulbs and rows of candles, cozy as a white sugar cave. The visitors are mostly with guides who reel off speeches learned parrot fashion in various languages; other men and women in religious garb offer candles, hustle you forward, beckon and wheedle, smile with sugary sweetness. You feel yourself distressingly harried by the mercenaries of religion.

All this architectural ugliness and spiritual vulgarity leads one's thoughts in desperation to Sabbatai Sebi and Jacob Frank, the followers of what G. Scholem, the eminent scholar in the field of Jewish mysticism, defines as "the deeply fascinating doctrine of the holiness of sin." As certain disciples of these strange masters sought salvation in killing, robbing, coming together in incestuous loves, invoking Supreme Purity in the depths of the cup of evil, here, too, one either flees in disgust or disposes oneself to savor the ugly, the worthless, the abject, hoping finally to distill from it some subtle catharsis.

Behind the rotunda of the Sepulcher is the Romanesque church of the Crusaders, mostly in the hands of the Greeks and therefore furnished with an impressive iconostasis. Recent restorations have re-established the original structure almost everywhere, and it has parts of great nobility—I am thinking particularly of the soaring central transepts just above the "world's navel."

Around the church itself is a whole ring of ambulatories. To the north is a very dark stretch known as the Arcades of the Virgin, which retains some portions of the oldest structures and offers a series of fascinating details. The Frankish architect, wanting to create some link between what was left of the old building and what was emerging of the new one, shaped certain parts of the roofing in irregular and asymmetrical forms which verge on sculpture. Arches and counter-arches, serving as a support, intersect one another surprisingly. One immediately thinks of that great sculptor of houses and temples: Gaudí.

Following the ambulatories all the way around, after going through the chapel of St. Longinus, the oratory of the Division of the Raiment, passing the stairs leading down to the Armenian crypt of St. Helena and, even deeper, the cave of the cross, one comes to Golgotha. Given the difference in level (fifty-odd feet) with the base of the church, the architectural solution was inevitably somewhat labored. Today

115

Church of the Nativity, belfry,
Bethlehem

there are chapels on two different levels, joined by steep, narrow stairs. Visitors can thus approach both the foot and the summit of the little hill where, according to traditions of the most venerable antiquity, the cross was erected. It was a place just outside the walls (Heb. 13:12), probably in front of the Gate of Ephraim. Apparently there were tombs and gardens on it. It was a particularly suitable place for capital executions; here the city was not profaned within its walls, while the proximity of the gate ensured the presence of a large number of spectators.

Today the hill—or what remains of it—is imprisoned within the walls of the Crusaders' church. Here and there small windows open onto this precious piece of earth. We are in the domain of the most intense popular religiosity. On the second floor there are two chapels, one beside the other, the Greek and the Latin. The Greek one is almost on the spot where, according to tradition, the cross was placed. In fact, visitors are shown a hollow in the rock which supposedly served as the base for its support.

The Greek chapel is aglow with light bulbs, oil lamps, candles; innumerable icons, side by side and indeed one on top of the other, cover the whole of the end wall; their silver frames glitter in concert with the gold haloes on the heads of the saints. It is all very festive. There is something affectionate and homely in the atmosphere that is most touching. You expect to be greeted by a plump, indulgent hostess with smacking kisses, and offered cakes. The reality of the everyday world, with its sharp corners, is here forgotten. A world of hieratically depicted saints lives in an empyrean all its own, in which you steep yourself as in a dream. You may interpret them as you please: as cosmic symbols, ideograms of a transcendent reality, or in terms of fable and legend, as sages or rulers, patriarchs and empresses, who came down to earth to bring good among men.

The Latin chapel, just beside it, seems bare and chilly in comparison; you are plummeted from mysticism to syllogism, from paradise to hard earth. Furthermore, the few works of art it does contain are concerned in their realism—suddenly almost frightening—with things which actually happened, which are still happening. They are not symbols to be read, like the Buddhas or Bodhisattvas in a Tibetan fresco, with reference to other realities. The man on the cross is history, chronicle, topography, the physiology of pain.

The place invites one, with the obviousness of a paradigm, to taste all the subtle differences of attitude, sensitivity, and style between the two main Christian worlds: Eastern and Western, Greek and Latin.

Coming out of the church of the Holy Sepulcher and following the walls around to the south, you can climb onto the roof of the building. It is up there that the Ethiopians have entrenched themselves. In the past economic reasons forced them to give up their position inside the church; they had to take refuge above, outside. And there they live in an extraordinary landscape of irregular cells and huts, some round like African ones, reminding one once again of Gaudi. Amid walls with surfaces shaped like shoulders and flanks of giants, rich in irregularities stressed by the oblique rays of the sun, studded with curious windows and twisting stairways and overgrown with a positive hanging garden, black priests appear, soft-footed and unexpected, smiling and unspeaking, tall and slender. If I really believed in thaumaturgy I would turn to them.

INDEX